Based on the true love story
of Florence and Guy Weadick
in celebration of the centenary of
the Calgary Stampede, 1912–2012

Florence LaDue fancy roping, 1912
Calgary Stampede

FLORENCE LA DUE.
WORLDS CHAMPION
LADY FANCY ROPER.

MARCELL PHOTO.

Wendy Bryden

THE FIRST

STAMPEDE

OF

FLORES LaDUE

A TOUCHSTONE BOOK
PUBLISHED BY SIMON & SCHUSTER

NEW YORK   LONDON   TORONTO   SYDNEY   NEW DELHI

Touchstone
A Division of Simon & Schuster, Inc.
1230 Avenue of the Americas
New York, NY 10020

First Touchstone export edition October 2011

TOUCHSTONE and colophon are registered trademarks
of Simon & Schuster, Inc.

For information about special discounts for bulk purchases,
please contact Simon & Schuster Special Sales at 1-800-268-3216
or customerservice@simonandschuster.ca.

Designed by Akasha Archer

Manufactured in the United States of America

1   3   5   7   9   10   8   6   4   2

ISBN 978-1-4516-0932-5
ISBN 978-1-4516-0934-9 (ebook)

This book is dedicated to the
most important women in my life

♦ Elizabeth Edgerton Copeland, my maternal great-great-grandmother, who (after her husband, Hugh Copeland, died) immigrated to Canada in the early 1800s from County Fermanagh, Northern Ireland, with her nine children, who were raised on her farm in Ontario. She died at the age of 100.

♦ Arabella Timmins Copeland, my great-grandmother, whose family was also from County Fermanagh, and who married James Copeland, the second son of Elizabeth and Hugh Copeland. They settled in Winchester, Ontario, and had eleven children, the sixth of whom (Sarah Jane) was my grandmother.

♦ Sarah Jane Copeland Dale, my gentle grandmother, who, despite always longing for the trees and water of the Ontario home where she was born, relocated as a young wife and mother to Red Deer in 1910, thus becoming the first Copeland woman to establish an Alberta branch of her Irish family.

♦ Ola Dale Carruthers, R.N., my beloved mother, who sparked my interest in writing so many years ago by giving me the bestselling autobiography *Why Shoot the Teacher*, authored by her Copeland cousin, John Victor Maxwell Braithwaite.

♦ Beryl Dowker Graham Bryden, R.N., a loving mother-in-law, who gave me a kind and understanding husband, whom I have loved over the years.

And most of all the beautiful and talented wives of our four sons:

♦ Lisa Bryden
♦ Kathleen Heddle
♦ Alexandra Ross
♦ Sarah Armstrong Bryden

and my granddaughters

♦ Wendy Ann Bryden
♦ Lyndsey Carolyn Bryden
♦ Lucy Jane Pepall Bryden
♦ Jessica Grace Bryden
♦ Gabriella Shae Bryden
♦ Beatrice Elizabeth Bryden

And, finally, to third-generation Alberta rancher

♦ Lenore Bews McLean, whose friendship with Florence LaDue Weadick provided the inspiration for this book.

Author's Note

Most of the stories about Florence and Guy Weadick were told to me by Lenore Bews McLean and were based on her own experiences and on tales that her mother, Josephine Bews, told her. My editor and I have taken the liberty of creating some dialogue for Florence and Guy, which I hope you enjoy.

And don't be confused—Flores LaDue Weadick was also known as Florence. Although neither of those is her original name.

Contents

CONTENTS

CONTENTS

THE FIRST
STAMPEDE
OF
FLORES LaDUE

The first time he saw her, Guy Weadick fell in
love with the upside-down Florence

PROLOGUE

The five horses probably outweighed her by a factor of fifty to one, and a kick from just one of their hooves could have killed her. But Flores LaDue, who weighed all of a hundred pounds and was barely five feet tall, wasn't afraid. She'd been around horses all her life and was as comfortable riding as she was walking. And she had practised her craft for years. Now was the time to show it off.

It was 1912, and Flores was performing at the first-ever Calgary Stampede. She had just impressed the crowd by roping a horse while lying on her back on the sandy Stampede infield. Now one trick remained before the awarding of the ladies' fancy roping championship. Flores rolled to her feet and assumed a narrow stance, just as her Mexican mentor, the legendary vaquero Vincente Oropeza, had taught her. The horse that she had already roped pranced about and circled her at a rapid canter. Suddenly four cowboys roared out of the gate; they manoeuvred their horses into a circle, and the other horse joined them. Flores motioned to them to ride their mounts out a ways, then turn them back toward her, five abreast. She stood silently, her back slightly arched. Then with a thirty-foot running start the horses began to gallop toward her at full speed. The ground trembled beneath their weight. The spectators hardly dared to breathe. But Flores was the very picture of calm. With flawless technique and timing, she made a series of five enormous flat swings and leaned out to spill the twirling loop where it belonged—around the throat latch—and snared all five horses.

With a magnificent championship belt and saddle, and the admiration of thousands, thus ended the first Stampede of Flores LaDue. Thankfully, for lovers of Western lore, it wasn't the last.

— CHAPTER I —

◆◆◆◆◆

Whisky and Wolfers— The Belle Epoque in Western Canada

Calgary City Hall, 1912
Glenbow Archives NA-1202-2

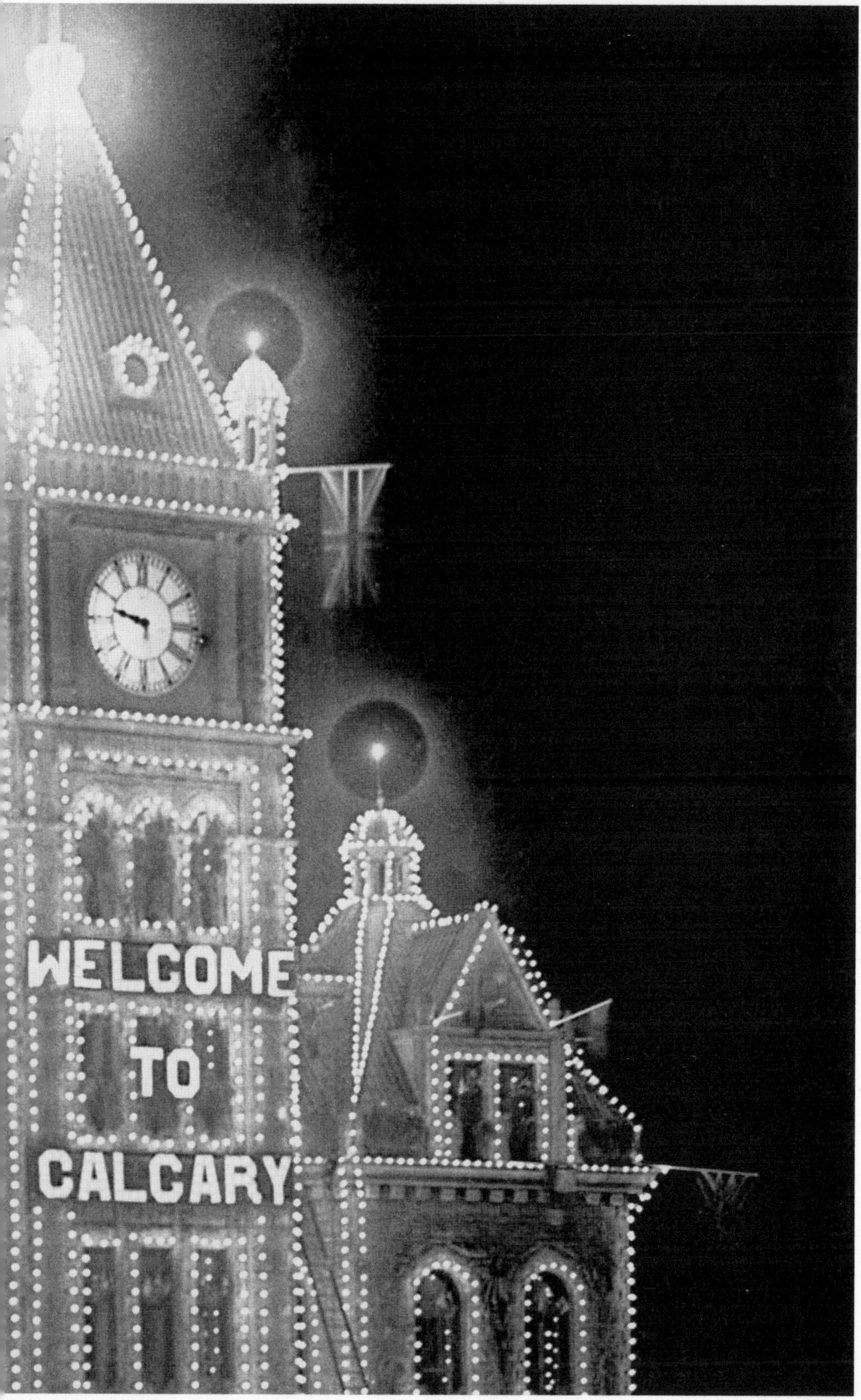
WELCOME
TO
CALGARY

Rodeo promoter Guy Weadick and trick roper and cowgirl extraordinaire Flores LaDue Weadick lived and thrived in a world of whisky traders and wolfers, a rough and tumble place that we have all seen represented in the movies, though it must be said that no mere film could ever capture the essence of Alberta at the end of the nineteenth century. As the Industrial Revolution was creating a class of industrial workers in Europe during the so-called Belle Epoque, the wild, romantic, cruel, heady, and impossibly beautiful Wild West of Alberta teemed with cowboys and Indians, and places with evocative names like Buffalo Jump, Empress, and Fort Whoop-Up, that last of which was the nickname of Fort Hamilton, a settlement that was established in 1869 near present-day Lethbridge. Fort Whoop-Up was one of the first trading posts in southern Alberta, an immense land that was then one of four provisional districts of the North-West Territories. All manner of goods were traded at the fort: buffalo robes, fabric, food, cooking utensils, guns, and, unfortunately for the Indian population, *napiohke*, white man's water—whisky— which brought such misery to the Blackfoot Nation.

In 1870, the Canadian government purchased the North-West Territories from the Hudson's Bay Company and secured the land in a series of treaties signed between 1871 and 1877. One American who was no doubt pleased that the land was now under Canadian federal government protection was a young American whisky trader named Fred Kanouse. In the spring of 1870, Kanouse and a ragtag collection of characters who shared a fascination with cowboy culture ventured into the northern-most point on the Whoop-Up Trail. There, on the north side of the Elbow River, Kanouse established a new post and con-structed a permanent building on land that later became Cal-gary. Kanouse and company were the first of a large group of Americans who trailed thousands of animals north from Texas to settle Alberta and produce the Alberta/American hybrid that, to this day, does not always ride easy in the harness of Canadian confederation.

The whisky-trading era finally came to an end in one of the most violent incidents in early western Canadian history, when a group of American wolfers massacred a group of peaceful Assiniboine Indians in the Cypress Hills Massacre in June of 1873. The wolfers were hunters who received money for every wolf they killed—since the buffalo had gone, timber wolves in the foothills had proved a nuisance to the early ranching busi-ness and were responsible for the loss of thousands of dollars each year. The incident at Cypress Hills spurred John A. Mac-donald, the Canadian prime minister who envisioned a Canada that reached from sea to sea, to secure quick passage of a bill to create a mounted police force that would police the region and guard Canadian interests. The force was modelled as a cavalry regiment and offered Macdonald his first opportunity to tame the land west of Manitoba. The new police force, outfitted in a traditional British uniform of scarlet tunic and blue trousers, stationed its first 150 recruits at Fort Garry, Manitoba. The following year, three hundred red-coated officers, who would become the North-West Mounted Police, left Dufferin, Manitoba, on horseback. Under the command of Assistant Commissioner James F. Macleod, the troops marched west for two months and subsequently established a permanent post at Fort Macleod, in the foothills of the Rocky Mountains, in southwestern Alberta. In 1875 the force sent troops north, and at the confluence of the Bow and Elbow rivers, they established Fort Brisebois (later renamed Fort Calgary), whose historic headquarters are preserved in the heart of present-day Calgary, not far from Fred Kanouse's operation.

No army can march on an empty stomach—someone had to feed those red-coated soldiers. The buffalo, which had been killed in mind-boggling numbers, were disappearing fast. This lack of animals sparked the rise of the now world-famous Alberta livestock business. In 1876, former Hudson's Bay employee George Emerson, who became known as the father of all Alberta ranchers, brought domestic cows from Montana north for sale and trade. Emerson, wisely keeping the majority of his herd to himself, set up operations near Calgary and commenced a small dairy operation that sold butter and milk to the Mounted Police, a ready market at Fort Calgary, also sometimes called the Bow Fort.

Fred Kanouse, who took up the stockman profession full-time and became the very picture of progress and respectability, would subsequently see these herds of cattle—some of which laid the foundation of the ranching industry on the immense open land of the three future provinces of Alberta, Saskatchewan, and British Columbia—move to a few large operations whose success was determined by the presence of water and the right topography, and whose owners would strive to contain their animals on their chosen range. He would also witness the arrival of huge corporate ranches such as the Cochrane and the Bar-U, wonder at the arrival of the Canadian Pacific Railway, see dusty cow towns become cities, and watch hitching posts give way to automobiles. Finally—with the exception of a few large fenced leases in Alberta's south and east—Fred Kanouse would watch the open range give way to fenced-off fields, and a particular way of life fade into a romanticized past.

Realizing the Romance— The Calgary Stampede Is Born

Kanouse was not the only one who felt a deep attachment to the Western way of life and who mourned to see the open range divided into ranches and farms. As a consequence, he would become involved in the first Calgary Stampede along with a larger-than-life rodeo promoter by the name of Guy Weadick, who happened to share his views. Indeed, it was Guy Weadick who had the vision to kick-start the Calgary Stampede, and his powers of persuasion came in at the right time when ranchmen George Lane, Patrick Burns, A. E. Cross, and Archie McLean, who would eventually be known as the Big Four, agreed to finance the first Calgary Stampede in 1912.

The Calgary Stampede has become an internationally known event attended every year by over a million people. They come to Calgary from all over the world to watch the fabulous Western shows and partake in the many Stampede traditions, such as

wearing the white felt cowboy hats that have come to symbol-
ize Calgary. And the grand parade that opens each Stampede
has become a beloved yearly spectacle. The parade in 1912 had
75,000 spectators, well more than the population of Calgary at
the time; today's parades have about 350,000 spectators, dozens
of marching bands, 170 floats, and hundreds of horses, cowboys,
cowgirls, clowns, First Nations dancers, and members of the
Royal Canadian Mounted Police, resplendent in red serge. And
there has never been a shortage of national and international
celebrities to serve as grand marshal of the parade: noted Hollywood personalities Bing Crosby, Bob Hope, and Walt Disney;
prime ministers Lester B. Pearson and Pierre Trudeau; former
Alberta premiers Peter Lougheed and Ralph Klein; Native lu-
minaries Chief Dan George, Blackfoot Chief Strater Crowfoot,
and Stoney Chief John Snow; "King of the Cowboys" Herman
Linder; astronaut Colonel Chris Hadfield; television personality
Mike Holmes; and even British royalty in the person of Charles,
Prince of Wales, have all taken a turn sitting in a vehicle or
riding a horse at the head of the 4.5-kilometre parade route
through the streets of Calgary.

Guy Weadick was a visionary. And there was no woman
more ruefully aware of his strengths and weaknesses, gifts and
curses, potential and problems, than his wife, Florence LaDue
Weadick, who, as a world-champion trick roper, had more than
a few strengths of her own. In fact, Florence was instrumental
in the making of her husband, and he was instrumental in the
establishment of the Calgary Stampede as the greatest outdoor
show on earth. It is no exaggeration to say that Calgary would
not be the city it is today if it had not been for the vision of both
Weadicks and the risk taking of the Big Four.

The first Calgary Stampede took place in 1912, but the Weadicks' story started long before that, when a young boy from the state of New York was seduced by tales of the Wild West and a precocious teenaged girl ran away from her home in Minnesota to join the circus.

CHAPTER 2

◆◆◆◆◆

Real Partners

Calgary Stampede grandstand, 1912

Glenbow Archives NA-1545-1

At the Calgary Stampede, 1950

"One man's junk is another man's treasure," declared Florence LaDue Weadick, sixty-seven, to Lenore Bews, eleven, as they huddled together in the grandstand.

Lenore looked at her quizzically. Florence realized that she needed to expand Lenore's Stampede education.

"I am talking about the chuck wagons, child. During the Civil War in the United States, army surgeons used wagons as operating tables," said Weadick. "Cowboys then converted them to food wagons when the West opened up after the war. If they hadn't, the wagons would have ended up in the junkyard, and we wouldn't be watching this great show today." It didn't matter that Lenore Bews had only the vaguest idea of what the U.S. Civil War was. A thoughtful and unhurried child, she was happy just listening to Mrs. Weadick and her tales of her career as a prize-winning, world-champion trick roper known by the exotic name of Flores LaDue, and of the exploits of her husband, Guy Weadick.

It was a piping hot day at the 1950 Calgary Stampede, and

dirt flew sky-high as teams of horses thundered round the final corner of the rodeo racetrack. Behind the horses came the boom of the chuck wagons, four wide across the track. The earth shook as tons of sweating horseflesh, outriders, and wagons crossed the finish line in a riot of colour. The race was over. Good money had won.

That morning at sunrise, Florence LaDue Weadick had picked up young Lenore Bews, the daughter of the Weadicks' next-door neighbours, Josephine and Joe, at their ranch southwest of Longview, in the old green 1927 Chevy pickup that the Weadicks used for hauling groceries and picking up guest luggage at the High River station for the drive back to the ranch. Tiny Florence could barely be seen over the pickup's steering wheel, and out of a sense of mischief, she always drove slightly over the speed limit. But that day there was an additional incentive for speed—she wanted to make it to the Stampede to tour the grounds and get to the infield in time for young Lenore to see the rodeo and the chuck-wagon races, which Calgarians affectionately called "the chucks."

Florence had never had any children of her own, but she had felt a special bond with Lenore from the minute she held her as a newborn, and she had vowed to herself to be a loyal and honest friend to the little girl. This proved to be an easy promise to keep; she found that she liked spending time with the youngster and often took Lenore with her on her rounds. Though this might sound strange to modern ears, in those days there were no babysitters for ranch wives. Often mothers plopped their babies and small children onto the saddle of a calm and reliable horse and tied them to the saddle horn to keep them out of harm's way. And when a mother had to take a horse out onto the range, the babies often came with them. Mrs. Bews knew that Florence loved Lenore as though she were her own daughter, and she was only too happy to relinquish her little girl to this master horsewoman. In fact, Lenore had been going out on the open range with Florence since she was a baby, riding on a tiny pillow on Mrs. Weadick's saddle, cuddled up between the warmth of her and the saddle horn. By the time she reached her second birthday, Lenore had her very own horse to help move the cattle, and by the age of six she had learned enough about roping from Mrs. Weadick that she herself was roping, wrestling calves, and helping to brand stock.

Mrs. Weadick had a deep understanding of and empathy for horses, and she taught Lenore to closely observe how they behaved and to distinguish between an Arabian, Morgan, registered Thoroughbred, and an Indian cayuse horse.

"Just like people," she told her, "they each have individual personalities. But more than that, child, they are godlike creatures. They did as much as any man to settle the West, and me and my husband would not be who we are today without them."

The little girl had already developed a love for the wagons at the High River Rodeo. What she didn't know, and what Mrs. Weadick now explained, was that chuck-wagon races dated to the fabled cattle drives of the late nineteenth century. Back then, cattle crews heading back from roundups raced the four-wheeled wagons, which were essentially kitchens outfitted with supplies, a water barrel, and cook's stove, for the last mile into town—the last chuck-wagon driver through the saloon door bought the winners a round of drinks. The Stampede's aptly named Half Mile of Hell owes its biggest debt to what must have been a wild scene. And more than that, although every ranch kid in Alberta, including Lenore, knew that Guy Weadick organized the first Stampede in 1912, what she didn't know until that day was that in 1923 Guy Weadick had fashioned the workaday cook wagon into a Stampede racing machine that became the chuck wagon. To everyone within earshot, Florence said, "That husband of mine had a darned good idea. Don't you think?" And she winked at her young charge.

Just then a voice blared over the loudspeaker.

"Ladies and gentlemen, this afternoon Mr. Dick Cosgrave, our own world champion with the most races ever won, is going to be one happy citizen of Rosebud, Alberta, when he awards fifty thousand dollars to Bob Heberling, the winning driver from his very own hometown. Now, folks, that is some good money," barked the infield announcer as thousands of spectators cheered the finals winner of the Stampede purse.

Florence and Lenore joined in the clapping and shouting, and the Stampede lessons continued with a few breaks until the day began to wind down and the stands to empty. They remained seated to watch the rodeo closing until a fellow in a suit and shiny hard boots pushed past them without so much as an "excuse me."

"Better watch where you are stepping with those boots, mister. Can't you see I have a child beside me?" Florence reprimanded. "I may be small but I'm not invisible."

At the mention of boots, Lenore leaned forward, her chin in her cupped hands, and gazed down with pride at the black tooled cowboy boots that Mrs. Weadick had given her. Western leather boots for children were not common, and Lenore Bews probably wouldn't have been wearing such a nice pair if Mrs. Weadick hadn't had such tiny feet.

Flores LaDue's boots

Mikael Kjellström, Museum of the Highwood

"If those boots are still comfortable, let's test them out with a walk over to the barns," said Mrs. Weadick. "I have access."

As they joined the throngs going down the stairs, they were among the few allowed through the inner gate bordering the infield. Several cowboys lifted their hats as they entered, nodding in respect. Mrs. Weadick not only had access, she had history behind her. She and Lenore walked hand in hand across the dusty infield, past the surrounding Indian tipis. They crossed the racetrack and entered an area consisting of a large group of agricultural buildings and horse barns along the south side of the Elbow River, around which much of the Stampede's operation revolved. The barns were well-crafted low structures built with a horseman's touch.

Inside, the dust spun silently in a wedge of sunlight. Everywhere, all the time, rose the earthy smell of horseflesh. As the two walked in, a cowpoke in his mid-forties looked up from a poker game and lifted a well-worn hat off his head. "Florence Weadick!" he shouted, jumping to his feet. "It's been a while." Lenore looked up at a man with a tanned face mapped with wrinkles and a lopsided smile.

"Hello, Herman. Still temptin' fate, I see," Mrs. Weadick said, gesturing at the card game.

"Oh, you know how it is, Florence. Don't tell these other guys, but I got a pair of aces in the hole."

"Your secret is safe with me."

"And who is this little filly, then?"

"This is my neighbour's daughter, Lenore Bews, and she invited me to take her to her first Calgary Stampede."

"Welcome, Lenore," he said. "Have a look around. You know, these barns are the heart and soul of the rodeo. But I imagine Mrs. Weadick already told you all about that."

Lenore was entranced. She looked around with wonder at the collection of bridles, ropes, chaps, boots, spurs, jackets, and gear as she walked along more saddle racks than she'd ever seen in one place. She stopped to rub her hand over a brown leather saddle, the most cherished possession of a rodeo cowboy. She took a deep lungful of a scent she had been smelling since she was a small child: the gorgeous mix of horseflesh and leather. Mrs. Weadick had taught her all about the various grades of leather and showed her how to recognize the better ones. "You've got to smell it, feel it in your hands, notice the texture, colour, and quality of the tanning so you don't waste your money on cheap imitations."

They were all set to walk over to see the wagons when from a distance came that old familiar whickering of the horses, and in perfect unison Florence Weadick and the little girl turned and walked toward the sound.

Lenore noticed that Mrs. Weadick's demeanour had changed; she had become pensive.

"The whole world is changing out there, Lenore," she said, "but in here, nothing has."

Florence took Lenore's hand and held it as they walked along the pens of rodeo stock; the broncs were uneasy in their confinement, pacing in their stalls, pawing the ground, and backing away at the first sight of anyone. As they passed the bucking and wild horses, she leaned down and whispered in Lenore's ear: "You just met Herman Linder, from Cardston, Alberta. He won twenty-two Calgary Stampede championships in ten years. He can ride anything that moves—saddle broncs, bareback horses, bulls. And he can rope calves with his eyes closed. No man has ever matched his record. And I bet no one ever will." Something else that would have amazed Lenore, if she had been able to see into the future, was that one day Herman Linder's daughter, Rosemarie, would marry Tom Bews, the most mischievous of Lenore's brothers, who was shy and tongue-tied in the presence of his hero, Guy Weadick.

Then with her trademark wink, Florence sank her hand into her Paris-designed handbag and extracted a bunch of carrots with shaggy green tops. She never went anywhere without the handbag that Guy bought her in 1911, when they were performing in France with Buffalo Bill's Wild West Show. "Now we have to go into another section of the barns," she said as she took a deep sniff of the carrot greenery, "and that's where we'll feed God's finest creatures."

They walked silently along the stalls till they reached some barrel-racing horses pawing the ground: "These are new to rodeo and draw a good cheque," she said. "Mr. Weadick and I always had good horses at the Stampede Ranch, with excellent blood-lines." She stopped to rub a velvety nose that had been thrust in her direction. "And I know a good one when I see it. This is Budger, and he's a quality animal. He wants to win, and that's the main thing for a barrel-racing horse. Strong and muscular is important, but a horse has to have a good heart—and a heart to win for the rider—and nothing is more important than that."

The woman and child listened to the gentle rhythm of horses breathing. They were both content with each other's company and did not feel the need to constantly chatter. Besides, for Lenore, just being with Mrs. Weadick was special, as though she were in on some kind of secret or had some kind of advantage over the other girls her age. And it was usually fun, too. She never knew what Mrs. Weadick would come out with next—whether she would tell a story or make a joke. "Call me cock-eyed," Mrs. Weadick said, rising to the tip of her toes to reach the latch of a door, "but I will guarantee that even if it takes fifty years, the purse for ladies' barrel racing at the Calgary Stampede will someday be upgraded to equal day money for the men's events. And why the hell not?"

Lenore's eyes widened. "You said 'hell,' Mrs. Weadick."

"My apologies for swearing, child." Florence turned to hide a smile. "I promised your mother I'd stop doing that."

She really was going to have to work harder at curbing her salty tongue around Lenore. She'd been trying to ever since one hot summer evening a couple of years before. She had been in-side the house getting supper ready. Through the kitchen window, she could see Guy talking to the hired hand for over an hour. She noticed that the hapless cowpoke couldn't get a word in edgewise with her husband, so she opened the window over the kitchen sink and yelled: "Goddammit, Guy, would you shut up! I'm not going to hold your dinner forever." Then she slammed the window shut and turned to see sweet little Lenore, who had let herself in the back door, standing with her mouth hanging open, stunned at the profanity issuing from the mouth of her paragon of virtue.

Florence opened the front door of Budger's stall, and the little girl entered fearlessly, which pleased Florence—it reminded her of herself as a young girl. Lenore walked gently forward, holding a carrot flat in her small hand. Swivelling its ears toward her, Budger leaned down to lip the carrot off her fingers.

Seeking Redemption

Florence's connection with these dark rooms teemed with memories, both good and bad. Back when her husband was Stampede manager, over 130,000 spectators attended the 1923 Stampede; by 1929, the attendance had risen to 258,000. But attendance dropped during the Depression, and the Exhibition board faced the deficit by cutting the budget. This had not pleased her husband, who had planned for the 1932 Stampede to be a huge twentieth-anniversary celebration of the extravaganza he had created. And, indeed, the 1932 Stampede had been the best one to date, but the directors had begun to resent Weadick's unpredictable behaviour and freewheeling attitude toward other people's money. Never one to deny himself alcohol, Guy Weadick's response to their criticism was to uncork and quaff half a bottle of Old Buck Rum on Finals Day, the consequence of which was that he lost all restraint. His bad behaviour reached a crescendo at the closing ceremonies, when, despite Florence's pleas and those of others, he could not be persuaded to stay off the platform. Officials had issued instructions to turn off the microphone if he disrupted the championship presentations in front of the sellout crowd, which he did. Thus it was that in the middle of a rambling speech that mortified Florence, Guy's microphone went dead. It took a moment for him to figure out what had happened. After he did, his embarrassment turned to anger. He grabbed a megaphone and to the upturned faces of all the cowboys, cowgirls, and spectators in front of the stage shouted: "I put on your first Stampede, and I've just put on your last!"

He was fired by the Exhibition board the next month and was never reinstated, though he later won a lawsuit for breach of contract and unfair dismissal against the board, which defended itself by stating that his drinking had disgraced his job. Guy would be the first to admit that he was a two-fisted drinking man, a rather common attribute in those days, but he denied that he was an alcoholic. In a judgement that people today might find outrageous, the judge sided with Guy, ruling that drinking was part of his job as Stampede promoter, and he awarded him six months' salary plus $1,700 in legal costs.

Florence and Guy hadn't set foot in the Stampede infield since that fateful day almost twenty years before. But this year Florence had heard talk that she and Guy were going to be invited back to the 1952 Calgary Stampede for its fortieth anniversary. She silently prayed that this would happen and that it would assuage her husband's feelings of betrayal. She dreamed that she and Guy would be asked to ride in the parade, and, once again, she could show her championship saddle, with which she had performed all over Europe, the United States, and Canada.

Almost all her wishes came true.

Winding Down

Stampede Ranch brochure, 1950s

McLean family collection

As their performing careers wound down, Guy and Florence stayed in Alberta and in 1920 bought a ranch west of High

River, which was both a working ranch and also a kind of dude ranch, the first of its kind in Canada. They called it the Stampede Ranch, and as time passed it became a gathering place for guests, friends, neighbours, and celebrities, and it had more memorabilia than they had places for. During the 1920s and '30s they were proud to have had three cowboy movies filmed on their land starring such famous Hollywood stars as Tom Mix, Hoot Gibson, and Neal Hart. Then, in 1928, Guy took the reins to shoot, produce, and act in an epic called *His Destiny*. "It was not the worst movie ever made," Guy noted at the grand opening at the Palace Theatre, in Calgary, as Florence, standing behind him, discreetly rolled her eyes, no doubt thinking, *But it sure wasn't the best.* They also counted among their many friends such people as Will Rogers, the well-known American cowboy and performer; Charles Russell, the famous Western artist; and the neighbouring Bews family.

Although Florence had always worried about Guy's drinking, all in all she was happy with her marriage, though her husband's romantic indiscretions sometimes severely tested her forgiving nature. She wasn't stupid—she knew that her tall, gregarious husband was attractive to other women. But she also knew that he would never meet anyone to match her and that he would always come back. And though she tried, she could never stay angry at him, though when he transgressed she made him dance to get back into her good books, and she often sat back, watching with what could almost be described as glee, as he fumblingly tried to extricate himself from various pickles with sweet words and gifts to placate her.

That was how she got the beautiful inlaid coffee table a few years after they first bought the ranch. He'd been seen escorting another woman in their 1926 Chrysler coupe. Rumours abounded about who the woman was and what Florence Weadick would do if she ever met her. There were also rumours that Mrs. Weadick had declared that she would never set foot in Guy's coupe again. And this rumour turned out to be true—for months after the rumours started, whenever they left the ranch to go into town, she made Guy drive ahead of her in his car and open all twenty-two gates. In those days ranchers needed the gates to keep their animals where they were supposed to be; there were no cattle grids, or Texas gates, which are depressions in the road covered by a grid of metal bars that are wide enough for animals' legs to fall through but narrow enough to allow vehicles to drive over them. The ranch hand who usually opened and closed all the gates at the Stampede Ranch was nine-year-old Oliver Perry, from High River, whom Guy Weadick hired in the summer to chop wood and help "Mother Weadick" (as he called her) with the chores. No one was faster at jumping out of a truck bed to open a gate than little Oliver. Guy Weadick would move his Capital model Chevy truck into low gear to drive through and by the time he'd thrown it back into second, Oliver Perry had closed the gate and had jumped back into the moving truck. But now it was Guy Weadick himself who was dealing with opening the gates, while back at the ranch, under strict orders from Mother Weadick, little Oliver Perry was chopping a mountain of wood and grooming more horses than he'd ever seen in his life.

Florence was a seasoned performer who knew more than a little about dramatic scenes. As a result of the rumours, she was in the kind of high dudgeon that could have qualified her for a role in one of the Western movies that had been filmed at the Stampede Ranch. So, to make her point, she would drive through an open gate in her own 1929 Ford truck and get out and close the gate in as dramatic a way as possible. Guy had hired Indians to fence his land with barbed wire. The Indians loved the Weadicks; in the spring they arrived from the nearby reservation with their children, wives, and dogs jammed into an old Democrat wagon pulled by a team of horses, set up their tipis beside the creek, and fenced almost all the land from High River to the Chain Lakes.

Florence still smiled whenever she thought of the day she was taking her own sweet time to close a gate as Guy watched her through the back window of his car, fuming. She was walking back to her truck when she looked up just in time to see poetic justice being delivered in the form of a splat of crow poop on his car's back window. Bird excrement obliterated the image of his face behind the window for a second, then it slowly began to drip down, revealing her husband's right eyeball levelled at her. What it saw was Florence doubled over, convulsed with laughter. The following day, the coffee table arrived at the ranch, and the usual fence opening and closing practices recommenced.

Over the years, Oliver Perry practically grew up at the Weadicks' ranch, and, in the process, he learned a lot about women, relationships, and the inner workings of major hotels, specifically, the ninth floor of the Palliser, a Canadian Pacific Railway Hotel, and, with its fifteen stories, the highest building in Calgary until 1958.

"Get in the truck, Oliver," Florence would say to him as the sun began to set and there was still no sign of her husband. "We're going to town."

And he knew that they would be headed for the Palliser,

where Florence would check the parking lot for Guy's 1926 Chrysler coupe. The scene tended to happen most often during the buildup to Stampede, when Guy would get distracted when dozens of his friends and cowboy contestants from Alberta, Arizona, Manitoba, Montana, New Mexico, Oklahoma, Oregon, and Texas arrived in Calgary and gathered in large suites on the Palliser's ninth floor. With Prohibition still the law in the United States, Guy Weadick was more than pleased to have the bars in the rooms stocked with genuine scotch and Canadian rye whisky. Indeed, along with another CPR hotel, the Hotel Macdonald, in Edmonton, the Palliser was one of the first two establishments to receive a liquor licence when Alberta abolished Prohibition in 1924. Just to be on the safe side, official Stampede cars with sober drivers were made available to cattlemen, old-time cowhands, and rodeo contestants. Once Guy Weadick started visiting with his friends it was hard for him to say goodbye, and as a result, Florence was left all alone at the ranch.

During the summer of 1928, just ten days before the Stampede was due to start, Guy Weadick was missing, and his wife knew where to find him. Once Florence Weadick's one-ton Chevy hit the paved streets of Calgary, Oliver Perry began to feel a tightening in his youthful throat as he saw the Palliser Hotel looming ahead. Sure enough, Florence roared up to the baronial entrance to the hotel, threw the truck into neutral, pulled on the emergency brake, and, leaving the truck unlocked and the keys in the ignition, hopped out.

"Come along, Oliver," she said, descending from the driver's side with a head of steam. "I need your help to get Mr. Weadick home."

Once in this grand hotel, they walked along corridors and looked through open doors into rooms cluttered with bedrolls, saddles, chaps, spurs, ropes, and the occasional husky body of a bronc rider. Yet an open door was not what Florence Weadick was seeking—she was looking for a closed one. She knew that in the room behind it half a dozen or so men would be passing the bottle, clowning around, arguing about judges' decisions, and telling good-natured lies. She found the room she was looking for and began pounding on the door, but the room's inhabitants either did not hear her over the noise they themselves were making or didn't care who was knocking. What did make them stop, though, was the crash of the glass of the transom breaking and the arrival in the middle of the room of a decidedly feminine cowboy boot. Guy Weadick took one look at the fancy boot lying on the floor surrounded by broken glass, and his face blanched.

"Gotta be going, boys," he announced as he stood and opened the door to reveal a wide-eyed Oliver and an unimpressed Florence.

"You're not kidding," she said. "And don't forget my boot."

And even though the ride back to the ranch that night was a bit frosty, Oliver, who was sitting between Florence and Guy, had had to suppress his laughter. He couldn't forget the amazing flight of Florence's boot through the transom or the look on either one's face—Florence's steely determined one and Guy's sheepish one. And he remembered that when Guy Weadick was teaching him how to chop wood Oliver had confessed that he was a bit scared of the axe, and Guy had said to him: "A real man shouldn't be scared of sweet bugger all."

But that night, after seeing the look on Guy's face, Oliver Perry learned different.

And it was probably just a coincidence, but the year of the flying boot was the Calgary Stampede's most successful to date: attendance records were broken and a profit of $35,000 was made from exhibits, horse races, and rodeo events.

$\mathcal{D}$uring the decade after Florence and Guy parted ways with the Calgary Stampede, they received and declined numerous, often attractive, offers to produce other rodeos, devoted more time to their guest ranch, observed the end of the vaudeville circuit as it gave way to moving pictures, and watched many of their contemporaries either retire or go out of business. It was during these times that the Weadicks and their ranch neighbours Josephine and Joe Bews took many road trips together; they went to Wyoming to visit Guy's brother Tom and his wife, Kitty, to Minnesota to visit Florence's father, and to other places in the United States and Mexico to see old friends. During these trips they took the time to write postcards to Lenore, who was delighted to find them in the postbox at the ranch. And it was on these road trips that Florence Weadick told much of her life story to her ranching neighbour, Josephine Bews.

Just before Christmas 1946, at the age of sixty-three, Florence was admitted to Holy Cross Hospital, in Calgary, for surgery on an enlargement of her thyroid gland. Their doctor had warned both of them to slow down. They were getting on in years; life on the ranch was starting to prove too difficult for their old bones, and they knew it was time to leave. Florence had called the Alberta foothills home for twenty years, and it took the heart out of her to walk away from the ranch, so they

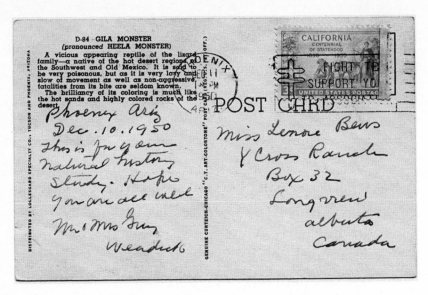

Postcard to Lenore from Florence & Guy Weadick, 1950

McLean family collection

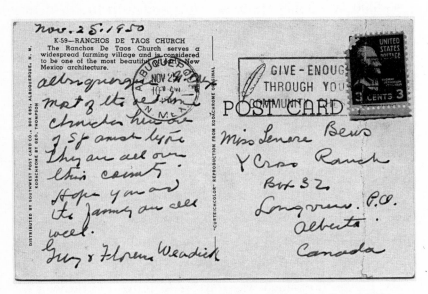

Postcard to young Lenore from Florence & Guy Weadick, 1950

McLean family collection

moved into a small house in High River, overlooking the foot-hills and the cemetery where her father was buried—after years of estrangement, the old retired judge left Minnesota to spend his final years with them on the ranch, and her reconciliation with him had been one of her proudest accomplishments. He had brought with him the little music box that her mother had left her. Before Florence and Guy sold their ranch, they gave the Stampede name back in consent with a prior copyright agree-ment with the Exhibition board, then they left for good on July 13, 1947, after Florence Weadick signed the guest book:

Name: *Flores LaDue Weadick*

Address: *The world*

Remarks: *The finest bunch I ever met*

She and Guy scouted for hot dry weather to improve their failing health, and by 1950, in time for their forty-fourth wed-ding anniversary, they settled in Phoenix, Arizona. They re-turned to Alberta twice: in the summer of 1950 to visit the Bews family (it was during this visit that Florence took Lenore to her first Calgary Stampede), and then again in June of 1951, for the dedication of the George Lane Memorial Park, in High River. Guy had felt obligated to be around for this event—after all, he had proposed the idea for the park in one of the many articles he had published in the *High River Times*. Florence's massive heart attack a few days after the dedication ceremony blindsided both of them, but she seemed to be recovering well at the hospital, so Guy was struck speechless by her death on August 9, 1951. He buried her beside her father and marked her grave with the simple inscription: A REAL PARTNER.

CHAPTER 3

♦♦♦♦♦

A Gift for Lenore

Guy Weadick

ENROUTE:

Phoenix, Ariz.
3401 E. Thomas Rd.
December, 11th. '51.

Dear Norrie:

I was delighted to receive your letter of the 5th. inst.,
this morning, telling of your many activities at the ranch.

I am sure you are doing a good job helping Mother and Dad
the way you are, while attending to your schooling at the ranch. It was
nice that your Aunt Ceclia was able to be there with you while your
Mother and Dad could take a little trip away, after their steady hard
work at the ranch all season.

I know as you grow older and look upon the days when you
were younger at the ranch, that you will be mighty proud that you
could have been such a help to your mother and father, and at the
samextime set an example for your younger brothers and sister as to
how ranch children should not only help their parents, but at the
same time learn all about livestock etc. that will be of great benefit
to them when they grow older, and how they can then teach their
children all about such things as they were taught on the ranch.

I Know Billy Joe is of great help to his Dad on the ranch
and I'm looking to see him do some mighty good calf heeling at the
branding next spring, if nothing prevents me from being up there.

It is coming on to Christmas and I have a present for
you that I know Mrs. Weadick would enjoy sending you were she here.
But it is impossible to send it satisfactorily owing to mail and
customs etc, so I will bring it up for you in the spring or early
summer when I come, and if anything should happen to me that I can't
get up, I'll see you receive it anyway. I am sure you will like it, and
I know that Mrs. Weadick would get much happiness were she alive to
join in with me in making the present to you. So while it will be
late, you will get it just the same.

I had a letter from your mother and dad while
they were in Montana, I have replied to it, before receiving
yours, for which I thank you. Every good wish to you and all
your brothers and sister and mother and father. Thanks for
your letter Norrie, and continue to study hard and help at
the ranch.   Your friend,

GUY WEADICK.

Miss Lenore Bews.
Y Cross Ranch.
Box 32.
Longview, P.O.
Alta.
CANADA.

Letter from Guy Weadick to young Lenore, 1951

Y Cross Ranch, West of Longview, Alberta, August 1952

Guy Weadick spent a lonely winter in Arizona. It was there that he made the decision to drive his one-ton 1927 Chevy truck back to the Highwood, southwest of Calgary. He had something he needed to deliver to Lenore Bews. And he decided that if he made it all the way back in his rickety old truck he would leave it with the new owners of the Stampede Ranch. It was a long trip driving in the slow lane of the highway in the old but reliable vehicle, but at last he crossed the border between Montana and Alberta and connected with the historic Cowboy Trail, now Highway 22, which ran north.

As he drove, he once again revelled in the glory of the sight of the Rocky Mountain foothills. The late afternoon sun caught the TS, the Stampede Ranch brand on the side door of the truck, as its wheels spun over the cattle guard at the entrance to the Y Cross Ranch, the home of his old friends, the Bews.

Up at the ranch house, the truck kicked up a cloud of dust that drifted into a nearby grove of lodgepole pines. He turned the engine off and pushed the door open with his left boot. Twisting sideways toward the passenger seat, he lifted a heavy saddle and heaved it over the steering wheel. Out of his truck now, he rubbed one toe of his cowboy boot against his blue-jeaned calf.

From her kitchen window, Josephine Bews watched the truck coming down the road and a few moments later opened the door to her tall lanky former neighbour. His still handsome face was sorrowful.

"I have something for Norrie," he said.

Josephine gestured for him to come into the kitchen, turned, and called, "Lenore, Mr. Weadick is here to see you."

Thirteen-year-old Lenore Bews was sitting at the dining room table, her head buried in her arms. She had been crying all afternoon—it was the one-year anniversary of the death of Mrs. Weadick. Her memories of the funeral were still very alive—she still remembered the sidelong glances she had received at the funeral for wearing the bright Mexican jacket that Mrs. Weadick had given her, though when one kind woman had complimented her on the beauty of the design, she had burst out crying. After the funeral, despite her father's and younger brothers' concerted efforts to cheer her up, she had remained inconsolable. Now, one year later, she was reliving every minute of it, but when her mother's voice called the Weadick name from their kitchen, her tears stopped.

She raised her head, wiped her tears, and got up from her chair. Taught good manners at the convent school that her parents sent her to in Pincher Creek, she wasn't about to be rude, especially to Mr. Weadick, the husband of the woman she had loved almost as much as she loved her own mother. Six years before, she had confided to Mrs. Weadick that she was horrified at the thought of going to the convent school and leaving her ranch and horses. That was when Mrs. Weadick gave her the pearl rosary that she would later twine into her bouquet in 1959, the year she married Roy McLean, and told her, "Go to school. Get an education, and then you will be able to do whatever you want." Since then, for Lenore, summers had been heaven sent, especially when the Weadicks stopped by the Y Cross three times a week on their way to town. So, on this August day in 1952, it wasn't unusual for Mr. Weadick to be at the Bews ranch. What was unusual was that Mrs. Weadick wasn't with him and never would be again.

Lenore entered the kitchen. As Guy Weadick turned to face her she saw that his eyes were brimming. "Lenore, if I can get it out, I'm just going to go ahead and say this." She had never seen Mr. Weadick, the fun-loving rodeo kingmaker, at a loss for words before. He struggled to continue: "Mrs. Weadick wanted me to give you her leather riding skirt and jacket. I brung it back

Flores LaDue's buckskin outfit

Mikael Kjellström,
McLean family collection

with me from Arizona." He moved the saddle toward her. "And she also wanted you to have her working saddle engraved with all her championship titles."

She touched the saddle. Her hands cupped the silver-rimmed horn reverently as she thought back to the first time she saw it—Florence Weadick had thrown it on her horse in the barn at the Stampede Ranch and exclaimed: "I always figure a horse likes the feel of a heavy saddle." Her diminutive hands had cinched it strongly before she'd stepped into the stirrup to mount. It was at that exact second—when her right leg was moving up and around the back of the saddle—that Lenore saw for the first time the engraved sterling silver plaque on the back of it:

FLORES LADUE

WORLD'S CHAMPION LADY FANCY ROPER

CALGARY   WINNIPEG   NEW YORK

1912–1919   1913   1916

RETIRED UNDEFEATED

More memories suddenly flooded back. Lenore remembered that earlier on the day that she had first seen the inscription on the saddle, breathless with excitement, she had run down to their barn to see Trixie, the new brown Thoroughbred Mrs. Weadick had given her for ranch work and for showing. She and Trixie had cantered over next door to thank Mrs. Weadick, who had suggested that they take the horses out. For half an hour they rode across the high open spaces of the foothills, not saying much, happy in each other's presence and comfortable in the quiet rhythm of the horses. They came to the crest of a cliff marked with sandstone outcrops, strange formations that had been sculpted by thousands of years of wind and water erosion. Millions of years ago receding glaciers had carved deep ruts into the windblown land, exposing the sandstone bedrock along the river valleys.

"The aboriginal people felt that the beauty of the coulees made them sacred, and they used them as places for spiritual gatherings," said Mrs. Weadick.

"Why do they call them *coulees*?"

"It comes from a French word, I believe, that means 'to cut.'

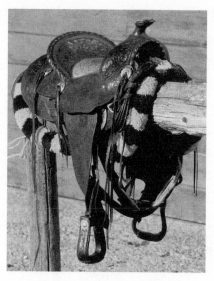

Flores LaDue's saddle

Mikael Kjellström, McLean family collection

Flores LaDue World Championship plaque

Mikael Kjellström, McLean family collection

Maybe it's because buffalo were run over the bank of a big hill into the coulees so they could be killed and cut to provide food, but they are also cool, quiet places for the animals to lie in the grass in the summer."

They zigzagged the two horses down the steep pathway, avoiding the spines of the thorny buffalo berry bushes, and reached the meandering Highwood River. The horses drank deeply before Mrs. Weadick and Lenore led them across the water at a shallow section downstream. Splashing out of the water, they rode up the opposite bank and arrived at the ridge, where they could see the red buildings of the historic Bar U Ranch nestled in the meadow below. The ranch was originally a 147,000 acreage leased in 1882 for a penny an acre from the Canadian government by the North West Cattle Company, a corporation managed by stockman Frederick Stimson and financed by the wealthy Allan family of Montreal. The level plateau and rolling hills of the plains supported tufts of native fescue grasslands, also known as prairie wool. The especially good forage of the rough fescue was particularly attractive to the early cattlemen, to say nothing of the sage growing in spots nearby, whose luxurious scent was carried on the wind. The frequent chinook winds that came over the mountains in midwinter blew away the snow and exposed these short grasses, thus making southern Alberta one of the few year-round grazing areas in Canada. Unfortunately for ranchers, this zone along the foothills also contained rich black soil that settlers ploughed under to seed crops, and once large-scale farming began, the range was never the same again. But on this day, with miles of soft undulating hills resembling whales breaching the ocean surface lying before them and the natural fescue grasslands passing under them, the old woman and the youngster had better things to talk about—horses.

"When I was your age, Lenore, I was forced to learn to ride English in a flat saddle, but I hated it and only did it to please my father, but all I ever wanted to do was ride bareback with the Sioux on a reservation in the northern plains."

The English saddle was flat, not curved like the western saddle, and it lacked a high cantle and saddle horn. Women, if they were ladies, were expected to use a sidesaddle, which allowed them to wear skirts and sit with their legs modestly together. To sit on a sidesaddle, the lady sat so that both her legs rested on the same side of the horse. Only women used such saddles in the North American West—regular western saddles were thought to be unladylike. Florence shuddered as she recalled the torment not just of riding English but of the fancy stiff riding clothes that went along with it.

"Before you gave me Trixie, I rode Indian horses too, so maybe they came from the same reservation." Indian horses were hardy bay mustangs, also called cayuse; they had thick manes and tails, and their legs were black from the knees down.

Where to start with this young girl, Florence asked herself. "I doubt it, child, because my Indian horses weren't raised in Alberta. They were raised in the United States, where I was born. That was way back in 1883 in a state called Minnesota, and, now that we're having this little talk, I might as well 'fess up that my real name isn't Flores LaDue or Florence LaDue or Mrs. Guy Weadick. My real name is Grace Maud Bensel."

Lenore Bews swivelled in her saddle, her small legs dangling on either side of it. "But why did you change your name, Mrs. Weadick?"

"It's a long story. I was born in a place called Montevideo, Chippewa County, in the American state of Minnesota. My mother died when I was just a baby. My father was a criminal lawyer, who later became a judge, and it was near impossible for him to raise an only child on his own. My grandfather was a government agent on a Sioux reservation close to town, so my father sent me there to grow up. The Sioux believe that a child is the greatest gift of all, and they welcomed me. But most important, the Sioux taught me how to ride horses. And from the very first day that I sat on a horse, I decided to spend every day of my life with them."

Florence paused to pat the side of her horse's neck.

"I lassoed and broke my own Indian horses and began to learn the tricks of roping. I liked roping because it was like a circle. Black Elk, the Sioux holy man, said I had made a good decision because even the seasons form a great circle in their changing and always come back again to where they were. Eagle Chief taught me that the One Above would not speak to me directly, but that he had sent me a horse, and from it I would learn many things."

"What did you learn, Mrs. Weadick?"

"Well, I learned patience, for one thing. I learned that if a person wants to have any success riding a horse, then they both have to be together in a spirit of cooperation, not conflict. And I also learned humility. Then, on one of my trips back to visit my father in Montevideo, I made a terrible mistake."

Lenore's eyes widened. What could this tiny perfect woman ever have done wrong? Florence paused to let the tension build; she had the instincts of a born storyteller.

"What did you do, Mrs. Weadick?"

"I told my father that I wanted to become a trick roper and rodeo performer. That was not the life he had envisioned for me, and he went sidewards on me. He said that it had been a mistake to send me to my grandparents and that I was spending way too much time on the Sioux reservation. He brought me back to town to go to school, and he tried to make a lady out of me by sending me to a local riding stable that didn't allow bareback riding. There, the owners told me that if I wanted to become a first-class horsewoman, the proper kind, I would have to learn to do everything. So I learned to clean out stables, I learned to groom horses, and I learned to ride English."

For several minutes, Florence was still. She looked west toward Longview, over the violet sheaths of the perennial bunchgrass. Cattle grazed on the bare open country that bordered the E. P. Ranch, which adjoined the Bar U and had once been owned by Edward, Prince of Wales. Prior to his abdication from the throne in 1936, Florence had actually taught him the basics of trick roping, and it had made quite a splash in the British press. But what was really in her mind's eye was the Sioux reservation where she had spent so many happy days as a child. Whenever she was out on the open prairie, she always longed to recapture those old feelings—the warmth she got when she leaned her forehead against a pony's flank, the feel of her heel in the weathered, cupped hands of her grandfather, and the soaring, upward movement when he hoisted her onto the bare back of her horse. She remembered racing her Sioux friends on their ponies, riding as though her shirttails were on fire, and the feel of her long black hair flying straight out behind her like a washboard.

"But, Mrs. Weadick," Lenore said, "you still didn't say why you changed your name."

Florence Weadick would hold on to the truth until the very last moment. How could she possibly explain her past to this innocent prairie child—a past that included performing for Queen Alexandra, the wife of King Edward VII; Empress Marie of Russia; and tens of thousands of Europeans? It would all sound too pretentious, even unbelievable. Better to start simple. "Well, child, since you ask, the reason I changed my name was because I ran away from home to join the circus."

"Lenore! Lenore! Are you listening to Mr. Weadick? We lost you. Where did you go just now?"

Lenore turned toward her mother: "I was just remembering the first day that I saw this saddle, and I was remembering what Mrs. Weadick told me when we went riding that day," she said, her eyes filling up again.

Guy and Josephine looked at each other. If anyone missed Florence more than Guy, it was Lenore. Guy knew that he had to find some consoling words for the young girl, something to ease her loss, and perhaps his own as well. After finding a spot on the oak sideboard for the saddle that held the folded leather clothes of Florence LaDue, he guided her toward the kitchen table. Then he sat down beside her and began to tell her about his Florence, or more properly, Mrs. Weadick—she would always be Mrs. Weadick to Lenore.

—CHAPTER 4—

◆◆◆◆◆

The Birth of
Flores LaDue

On her own, an apprehensive
yet determined
Grace Maud Bensell, with
a new identity, circa 1909

McLean family collection

BEAUTY

Montevideo, Minnesota, 1891—1898

In 1891, Grace Maud Bensel was eight years old when she first heard her father, Charles, mention the word *vaquero* after he read it in a newspaper article in the *San Antonio Daily Express*. She was home from the Sioux reservation for Christmas and was standing quietly in the hallway outside the drawing room of their Montevideo house; lightly, she tiptoed toward the light and put her eyeball up to the crack between the door and the frame. She was supposed to be in bed but had sneaked back to listen to her father and his houseguest, Colonel Fred T. Cummins, talk about the growing influence of Hispanic cowboys in touring Western shows. She loved it when Colonel Cummins came to visit; it was the best thing about being home. A long-time personal friend of her father's, Colonel Cummins had grown up among the Natives and developed his Wild West and Indian Congress into a travelling exhibition featuring aboriginal peoples. His tales about cowboys, traders, prospectors, and vaudeville were the stuff of grand adventure, and Grace was entranced. She heard her father mention an interview with the Mexican roper Vincente Oropeza, then billed as Wild Bill Cody's "Chief of the Vaqueros." In the interview, Oropeza, a cattle driver who specialized in trick and fancy roping, explained that the word *vaquero* was the Spanish word for *cowboy*; it was derived from the word *vaca*, which means *cow*. Oropeza was adamant in the interview—the Spanish word came first, and the English word *cowboy* came later, as a translation from the Spanish.

"I am not too sure about that," said the judge. "The word *cowboy* has been around for a good while."

"You are right about that, Charles, but we must admit, the cowboy tradition does come from Spain and their hacienda tradition. And we both know that horses are not native to this part of the world. The Spanish brought them, too."

"You got me there, Fred."

"And there are even more words for *cowboy*," said Cummins. "*Buckaroo*, for example, which I understand is also related to *vaquero*. *Cowpoke*, *cowhand*, and *cowpuncher*. In any case, it does not really matter where the word comes from. Our American cowboys mostly call themselves riders and are a highly unique breed." He paused. "And speaking of unique, how is that daughter of yours?"

Grace almost fell from her spy post.

"I swear, I don't know what to do with that girl, Fred. I sent her out to live with her grandparents on the reservation—I can't look after a girl child on my own, you know that—and the next thing I know she is riding all over hell's half acre, bareback, like a wild Indian brave. She will soon be a young woman, Fred. How is she ever going to find a husband if she carries on like that? I don't mind admitting, I am at my wit's end with Grace."

By this time, unbeknownst to her father, Grace had picked up some roping tricks from her Sioux friends and even had her own lariat, even though her father had forbidden it. In fact, she never went anywhere without it and tucked it into a corner of her carpetbag whenever she travelled between the reservation and Montevideo.

Despite her father's criticisms, Grace continued spending time on the reservation but she carried on with her schooling, too, even if she did so grudgingly. She also continued to practise her rope tricks and had accumulated an amazing repertoire. Although she was agile, Grace was also petite, and it annoyed her that people underestimated her abilities, especially her father. With each passing year, she would measure her height against her Sioux brothers and sisters of the same age, and each year she fell further and further behind them in height. This disadvantage bothered her intensely until she became a teenager and learned that one of the greatest monarchs of all time, Queen Victoria, was under five feet tall. If such a short woman could be the Queen of the United Kingdom and Ireland and the British Commonwealth and the Empress of India, if she could ride horses, be married to a prince, give birth to nine children, survive assassination attempts, all the while leading the government, then there should be no stopping Miss Grace Maud Bensel. From then on, the little girl without a mother of her own became a voracious reader of stories written about accomplished women. And over the years, she grew into a very determined young woman who did not take kindly to anyone mentioning the thorny question of her size.

Grace's life continued its usual pattern; she divided her time between the reservation and home, and her father continued to worry about her marriage prospects. Then, in her mid-teens, an event occurred that would change her life forever—the travelling circus came to town. And she was determined to see it.

"Deviltry! I forbid you to even go near it!" Judge Charles Bensel had thundered when Grace Maud asked for permission to go to the circus. Despite her pleading, her father would not bend, and she eventually agreed to obey his dictum, even though she knew deep down that as soon as he left the house, so would she.

And so it was that Grace Maud Bensel, despite her father's best efforts, fell in love with Wild West shows. For the first time in her life, she witnessed the hair-raising, spine-tingling stunts of an amazing assemblage of Indians, vaqueros, Cossacks, and vaudeville performers, including Will Rogers, the famous American cowboy, humourist, and vaudeville performer. And the horses! Thoroughbreds, standardbreds, and Appaloosas. Never had she seen such an outstanding and beautiful group of horses, all performing feats with their cowboys. During that first circus, as she stood in awe beside the sawdust ring, she knew what she wanted to do for the rest of her life.

After the show, she approached Will Rogers. "I would like to audition," she told him. "I can rope with two ropes at a time." He looked at this tiny brunette who appeared to be no more than fifteen or sixteen with a mixture of surprise and admiration, and the look doubled after he saw what she could do with a rope. He knew that roping with two ropes was difficult for a lot of cowboys—he didn't know any women who could do it.

"Young woman," Rogers had said to her, "are you sure about wanting to join the circus? I see that you can handle a rope better than just about anybody I ever saw, but this is no easy life.

In fact, I sometimes question the soundness of mind of people who spend the best part of their life making rings with a piece of rope and going through life trying to jump through 'em, then when they get through to the other side, they immediately want to get back on the side they just come from."

Grace had never been more sure about anything in her life.

And so it was that that very afternoon the doors of a circus swung wide open to admit a petite brunette with lightning-fast wrists and an iron will. Circus management didn't know, though, that their new young charge came with some impressively heavy baggage in the form of her large and decidedly hostile father.

Grace Maud was afraid of no man but Judge Bensel, but as with swimming, she felt it was better to simply dive into the water than to pussyfoot around.

"Like Hell you're joining the circus!" he shouted at the dining room table that night, indifferent to her pride in her successful audition. "No daughter of mine is going to run off with a load of cowpunchers and Cossacks to join a circus. And do you know what that will do to your body? All that twistin' and turnin' will tear you up inside. You will never be able to have children if you carry on this way!"

Judge Bensel was echoing the popular wisdom of the day, which held that women should not sweat or get dirty, let alone ride around on horses, lest they damage their reproductive organs. Before she could even formulate a retort to this, the judge thundered: "Even if it kills me, I intend to make a lady out of you, Grace Maud. A proper lady."

What did it mean to be a lady, anyway, Grace wondered. Did it have to do with the way one spoke or acted? She had been looking after her father since her mother died—she could cook and sew as well as anyone. Did that qualify her to be lady? Was it the way a woman dressed that made her a lady? After her bath that night, Grace donned the frilly petticoat her aunt had given her for Christmas, but she still didn't feel like a lady. She sat on a rocking chair in front of her full-length bedroom mirror, took one look at herself, and began to bawl. "I am ugly as an ape," she cried, as tears rolled down her cheeks. But her tears were mixed with resentment and anger. She hated her father for his obstinacy, his bullying, and the way he failed to understand what made her happy. She hated school in Montevideo, she hated English riding, and she hated the thought of being a so-called lady.

The next day was Saturday, when the housekeeper, the hired hand, and her father always took the buckboard into town for supplies. As she sat alone in her room, a scheme began to form in her mind. She needed to make a getaway, and she needed to do it soon—the very next Saturday seemed as good a time as any. During the week that followed she mentally packed, deciding which items she would *not* take, such as all the engraved silver that her father said was hers, her schoolbooks, her school uniforms, her English riding boots, her jodhpurs, and the little silver music box her mother had left her. And which ones she would—her lariat, her ankle-length split riding skirts, her gingham scarves, her black Stetson, and any loose change she could find.

And she knew who her accomplice would be—her best friend, a young Sioux named Red Crow, who had left the reservation and moved into Montevideo, where he got a job driving a stagecoach. In fact, it was Grace's Indian agent grandfather who had signed the card allowing him to do so. Red Crow had become embittered. He said that the white man had taken territory that did not belong to him and pushed the Indians into a small corner, making them prisoners in their own land. Despite his resentment against white society, though, he liked Grace Maud. He knew that she loved his people and that she, too, mourned the loss of the open plain. For her part, Grace knew that she could trust Red Crow with her life.

The following Saturday morning, Red Crow drove up in a cloud of dust; Grace was outside the house waiting for him. It looked to him as though she'd been crying, but he had learned the hard way that she wasn't interested in pity or sympathy, so he silently jumped off the buckboard and yanked the side door open so she could throw her carpetbags onto the coach floor. He would take them to the circus, where she would pick them up later. They exchanged glances but said nothing to each other, and Grace was already running up the front porch stairs as he pulled away from the house. She took a broom that was propped up against the porch railing and ran with it down the stairs and along the path leading to the front gate. There she stopped to survey the tracks the wagon wheels had left in the dust. "Brush those away so they don't leave a trail," she whispered to herself, "and it will look like you disappeared without a trace."

Red Crow knew much about silence. That night, he moved like a cougar in the tall grass around the Bensel house. He got the ladder from the barn; it was exactly where she said it would be. He propped it up against the wall of the house, its top just under Grace's bedroom window. She silently slid onto the top rung of the ladder and climbed down. Once she was on the ground, Red Crow calmly returned the ladder to the barn. Then, without speaking, they walked through the dark shadows all the way to the gate of the circus grounds, where an official was waiting to let her in. Tears welled up in their eyes as they took leave of each other. Red Crow knew that he would never see her again, though he certainly would hear of her, only he would not know it was her—to prevent her father from finding her, Grace Maud Bensel needed to change her name. She had thought about a good stage name for a while and settled on something she thought sounded exotic and beautiful. She took the Spanish word for *flowers* and added a sort of continental last name that she liked, and thereafter she was known as Flores LaDue.

CHAPTER 5

◆◆◆◆◆

Roping Her Way to Fame, 1898–1904

Flores LaDue throws a loop with one
hundred feet of rope . . . a lot of rope
for anybody, especially a cowgirl
McLean family collection

In 1898, the newly christened Flores LaDue was a simple circus entertainer on the periphery of fame, though her dazzling talent would soon thrust her into the limelight—shortly after she joined the circus troupe, it merged with Buffalo Bill's Wild West and Congress of Rough Riders of the World Show, which was an internationally recognized Wild West extravaganza. Each Buffalo Bill show began with a horseback parade that included hundreds of soldiers, Indians, and a panoply of performers from abroad: Turks, gauchos, Mongols, Arabs— each displayed their own horses and distinctive costumes. Famous Western figures joined in, too. People like sharpshooter Annie Oakley, and famed Métis leader and marksman in his own right, Gabriel Dumont. The performers would stage such acts as re-enactments of the pony express and stagecoach robberies, and the culminating event was a notably melodramatic re-enactment of Custer's Last Stand at the Battle of Little Bighorn, in which Buffalo Bill himself played the part of the ill-fated general.

In addition to all these notable people, the show featured one of the most famous vaqueros on the circuit—none other than the renowned Mexican roper Vincente Oropeza, whose name Flores had first heard through a keyhole in her family home. Oropeza came by his skill honestly—fancy roping originated among the *charros*, another word for cowboys, of Old Mexico, where it was known as *floreo de reata*, or "making flowers of rope." Oropeza introduced trick and fancy roping into the United States in 1894 and won the first world roping championship in 1900.

"I've heard all about you," Flores told him upon being introduced.

Oropeza must have found it odd that this petite young woman not only knew about him but was even at the circus in the first place. Who was she? Where did she come from? Why did she have a Spanish name when she clearly could not speak a word of the language? But more to the point, how did she learn to handle a rope like that? He began to ask her these questions, but Flores was evasive—the last thing she wanted was for her father to discover her whereabouts and come after her now that she was experiencing her first taste of freedom.

Oropeza soon took Flores under his wing. One day in the early morning mist of an Idaho prairie spring, they were practising rope tricks on horseback in the show ring. "Buffalo Bill gave me the opportunity to become a trick and fancy roper in America," said Oropeza, who could rope ten calves at one throw, "so I think that it's time I share my good fortune with a young roper."

Oropeza was a most fashionable creature: all chaps, rope, sombrero, flowing moustache, and charm. Flores loved his gracious ways and the sound of his Mexican accent and how he always pronounced the letter *m* like an *n* at the end of a word. Manoeuvring his horse as though it were his waltz partner, he worked its reins through figure eights, straight runs, sliding stops, and 360-degree spins. Then he stopped to circle Flores in the ring: "Best thing about fancy roping is that you and your horse work as a teen (team)," he said, never taking his eyes off her. "You do not have to subdue the animal." This wasn't true for the runaway horses that the Mexican excelled at catching—he could lasso up to eight in a single throw.

Oropeza drew their two horses together to demonstrate how to tie a knot to form an eye. With lightning speed, he rotated various tricks across his body, as he explained the importance of staying clear of the ground and dilating a section of a spinning rope into a loop. Then he shifted his body to the side of his saddle and performed a couple of stunts as he rode upside down.

Flores was mesmerized.

"The centrifugal force of the loop will keep it open in midair as long as you keep revolving it," he conversed with the atmosphere, "but the rope has to be whirling before you cast it."

Did she just witness the initials of his name flying loop-by-loop across the sky? "That is my signature closing act," he said, "but first I think we should start with something less fancy, like the Wedding Ring."

"No use me learning that. I'll never get married. Men don't like me."

"Why do you say this, Flores?" he asked, puzzled.

"Too independent and too good a rider," replied Flores, who could spot a man suffering from chronic *lariatitus* a mile away, "and a man will be even more afraid of me when I develop too strong a muscle in my roping arm." *Lariatitus* was a word she had invented to describe men who feared her talent and strength, the kind who preferred their woman at home in the kitchen, cooking their supper for them. And, by George, she'd met more than a few of them.

Oropeza was at a loss for words. His realm was one of horses, ropes, sawdust; he knew nothing about women, let alone highly spirited and fiercely independent teenage girls.

"It is possible to attempt each of these tricks in the other direction," he said, "if you spin the Butterfly from the opposite direction with the rope turning counterclockwise." He paused and smiled. "And if you learn to do these tricks with your left hand, that will balance the muscle in your roping arm."

Flores continued to practise, generally keeping to herself when she wasn't taking lessons from Oropeza. The Wild West folks kept a blind horse that she used for practise—she called these sessions her "up and over roping parties for one." They also kept an old horse to deliver provisions to cold storage, and Flores took every opportunity to borrow him to practise opening the loop—getting the rope under control before she threw it over the horse's head.

Flores learned to love her gentle Mexican mentor and wanted to please him, so she practised relentlessly. Before long she had mastered many tricks: the Butterfly, Zigzag, and Ocean Wave. "Be quick, but don't yank the spoke," Vincente Oropeza would say to her, as she learned the Roll Overs. "The lift is an exact movement you have to learn to feel when you throw the loop up."

During the winter months, the vaudeville circuit was staged inside, but in the summer, Buffalo Bill's Wild West Show was held in enormous fields and, at every stop, attracted more and more people from the town and surrounding ranches. The railways brought in Pullman sleepers and laid sidetracks for the mobs of spectators that streamed in from every direction. Flores LaDue, now a young woman of twenty-one and not even five feet tall, was fast becoming one of the most crowd-pleasing performers. As for Oropeza, he was no longer with the Buffalo Bill show full-time. The previous summer Colonel Fred T. Cummins had offered him a job with his Wild West and Indian Congress, which he had expanded to include broncobusters, rope spinners, and cowboys of the generation before. On one of their last roping sessions together, Oropeza told Flores that she'd made good and that he was proud of her, and she told him that he had helped her make the impossible possible, and they had taken a fond farewell of each other.

All that said, although Flores LaDue was starting to enjoy her fame, she was lonely and often second-guessed herself. Will Rogers's comment about jumping through hoops echoed through her mind sometimes. And she wondered about her father. How was he? Was he coping without her? Did he hate her? Had she made the right decision, giving up a normal life to go on the Wild West circuit? She'd been with the show for over six years, yet had no man in her life and no faith that there ever would be one. Maybe her father was right; maybe her not being a lady meant that she would never have a husband.

Despite Flores's personal insecurities, her years of determined practise had paid off and she had no insecurities on the professional front—by this time almost no one could match her fancy roping exhibitions, and she wasn't doing too badly financially. Indeed, prize money was the bait drawing more and more women to the Wild West shows from one end of the United

States to the other, and from Canada, too, including such places as Calgary, Medicine Hat, and Winnipeg.

Some of the more well-known women on the circuit were Fannie Sperry, Bertha Kapernick (later Blancett), Goldie St. Clair, and Tillie Baldwin, a Norwegian who had competed in a variety of sports before she moved to America, where she joined the generation of young professional cowgirls now taking part in relay races and bronco riding. Baldwin had warned Flores to get rid of her riding skirt in competition. "Garters will keep you from courtin' death," said Baldwin, whose billowing pantaloons were "bloomered" by elastic armbands placed just below the knee of her split skirts. "My clothes give me a competitive edge and get me judged with better scores."

In the dusty business of rodeo, Tillie Baldwin's bloomers, which drew plenty of compliments from fellow riders, bucked conservative attitudes to women wearing trousers, but more than that, they were extremely practical. In fact, they would revolutionize performances for women trick riders. This was still the Victorian era, and women were expected to dress with modesty. The convention of the time called for floor-length skirts that completely covered a woman's legs—even showing an ankle was thought to be provocative, but obviously trick riders could not wear skirts. Imagine what would happen if a cowgirl wearing a skirt performed a headstand on a horse. Necessity being the mother of invention, a compromise was reached, and soon split skirts, or California riding costumes, were developed. Made of horsehide and sheepskin, they were a cross between skirts and pants.

From her childhood on the reservation to her performances in the professional ring, Flores LaDue was equally talented at both trick riding and trick roping. Yet her preference was for trick roping and that fact enabled her to wear her long divided skirts until the day she died. As fate would have it, she would eventually find a man who wanted to wear the pants, and that would suit her just fine.

CHAPTER 6

◆◆◆◆◆

An Irresistible Force Meets an Unimpressible Object

Young Guy Weadick,
circa 1905

Glenbow Archives NA 446-98

By the age of twenty-two Flores LaDue had been with the Buffalo Bill show for a season or two and was happy there; it had become home to her, and she knew every blacksmith, carpenter, harness maker, horse trainer, and ticket taker in the show. But she was beginning to hunger for something different. And soon the chance for a change presented itself—one day in 1905 Colonel Fred T. Cummins, her father's old friend and frequent houseguest, offered her top billing in his Wild West and Indian Congress, on the recommendation of Vincente Oropeza. Flores heaved a sigh of relief after her brief interview—he had failed to recognize her as the daughter of his old friend, Charles Bensel.

She joined Cummins's Wild West and Indian Congress in September 1905. At that time the company was playing an engagement in Chicago. During Flores's closing act, the moveable corral that was suspended up in the drops like painted theatre scenery would be lowered around her so that the bucking broncos could be brought in next. Her final act and the lowering of the corral took place simultaneously, and because there were no bleachers, the spectators standing on the sidelines moved forward to circle her in the infield. Sitting on her horse, she'd throw a large loop, then hook her right foot deep into the stirrup, pivot in her saddle, and like an inverted bow, arch backward to hang over the side of her horse. Later that year on a fine autumn day, she was in her downward arch, squinting at the sun and listening to the sound of her rope testing the air, when she caught an upside-down glimpse of a pair of smiling dark brown eyes beneath the rim of a ten-gallon Stetson.

Though she didn't know it at the time, she had just seen her future husband.

Guy Presumes

Guy Weadick was born in Rochester, New York, on February 23, 1885. The eldest son of a large family, he was hooked on the cowboy and Indian stories told by his uncles when they visited from the great cattle ranges of California, Montana, and Wyoming. He'd seen every Wild West show that had ever come to Rochester and was so enthralled with the West that upon the death of his mother in 1899, at the tender age of fourteen, Guy Weadick ran away from home to become a cowboy in Montana.

He first visited Canada in 1904, when he accompanied a horse trader to Standoff, Alberta, south of Fort Macleod. There, he witnessed his first Sun Dance Ceremony, the spectacular annual gathering of the First Peoples of the plains and the foothills. On his vest that day, he was wearing the latest Western fashion—a button with his photograph reproduced on it. Crop-Eared Wolf, chief of the Bloods, took a fancy to it so Weadick gave it to him as a gift. The chief proudly wore the badge till his death, and whenever he was asked who the man in the photograph was, the chief would reply: "This is a picture of my son."

Guy Weadick returned to Alberta the following year with his sidekick, Will Pickett, to introduce bulldogging, also known as steer wrestling, to spectators at the Calgary Exhibition, which at that time was an agricultural fair. It is said that Pickett originated bulldogging by accident when he dropped a pack of tobacco and stooped down from his horse to retrieve it. A thousand-pound wild steer charged him, and he wrestled it to the ground. In another version, an unruly longhorn steer got on Pickett's nerves so badly that he snapped: he rode alongside the longhorn, jumped onto its back from his horse, and grabbed its horns. The steer fought back until Pickett bit its lower lip, which rendered the steer docile, at which point Pickett wrestled it to the ground.

After the 1905 Calgary Exhibition ended, Weadick and Pickett headed to Winnipeg. Unfortunately, one night horse thieves made off with the stock that they had penned in the corral; the two men tracked the thieves to Montana, where the culprits were arrested, but legal red tape delayed the shipping of the horses back to Canada. At that point, Weadick and Pickett decided they needed a holiday, so they travelled to Chicago to catch the Cummins Wild West and Indian Congress Show, which was being featured at White City, a one-of-a kind park in Chicago that billed itself as a summer pleasure centre dedicated to merriment and mirth. White City featured a quarter of a million lights and buildings made entirely of white cement. In the centre of the grounds stood an electric tower with 20,000 incandescent lights and a powerful searchlight. Cummins's Indian Congress and its 150 Indians and cowboys provided entertainment in the form of a re-enactment of Custer's Last Stand.

Guy returned to Canada, to Winnipeg, to be more precise, to sign a contract to stage a Wild West show there the following year. Eager to secure bookings for Will Pickett, the one and only rodeo act he had in his arsenal, he returned to Chicago. This would prove to be a life-changing trip, for it was in this Illinois city that Guy Weadick would just happen to lock eyes with a young woman who was hanging upside down off the side of a horse, swinging a lariat, and his fate would be sealed. Guy Weadick had always had an eye for talent. And the day he saw Flores LaDue in Chicago, he knew that she was, far and away, the best finished product he'd ever seen.

It would be another year before he found his way back to make her acquaintance. By October 1906, he'd completed his contract to stage a Wild West show in Winnipeg and headed south to Iowa with Pickett to join up with Colonel Cummins's show. He was looking forward to it for a number of reasons: the Colonel's Wild West show was popular, and Guy stood to make some decent money. Plus, there was the memory of a certain dark-haired young lady who could throw a mean rope. Weadick had never forgotten her. Now all he had to do was find the young and, hopefully, still single Flores LaDue and persuade her that her days as a spinster were numbered. Between then and now lay the details.

He got off to a bit of a rough start when Colonel Cummins eventually introduced him to Flores: "Pleased to meet you, Miss LaDue. But haven't we met before?"

"I don't believe so." Flores was wary.

"I do believe I saw your act last year, in Chicago." Though Flores's show had been impressive, Guy was probably one of the few spectators who saw its flaws: her left leg was at right angles to her right one, and her skirt, which fell to either side, split right at the centre of her body.

"I couldn't help but notice you looked a little precarious on that horse. I would be happy to give you some pointers on—"

Flores was outraged at the presumptuousness of this smooth operator standing before her wearing chaps and a smirk. And years on the circuit had made her prickly.

"You have pointers for me? I have been riding hoses since before I could walk. With the Sioux of Minnesota, I might add, the best horsemen on the plains. Just what do you think you could teach me, Mr. . . . Mr. . . . what did you say your name was?"

"Guy Weadick, ma'am."

"Well, Mr. Guy Weadick—"

"I know it's presumptuous of me, Miss LaDue, but might I ask how old you are?"

"How is that any of your business?"

"It's just that this vaudeville life can be hard, and you look no more than sixteen years old to me, Miss LaDue, and perhaps in need of some protection."

Flores could feel her fury increasing by the minute.

"Don't you worry about me, Mr. Weadick. I have been look-ing after myself for a long time. And though it is none of your business, I am twenty-three years old. Now I have a question for you. Where are you from? You don't sound like you are from around here."

"I am originally from the state of New York—"

"New York!" She guffawed. "Oh, yes, you must be one of those famous New York cowboys that I have heard so much about. And might I also ask, just what are you doing here?"

"I've just been hired by the colonel to bring Will Pickett's bulldogging act into the show." His eyes patrolled her. "I think I am going to like it here." He was certain that he saw her blush, but then she took him by surprise.

"Nice making your acquaintance," she said, as she turned on her heel, "but don't be surprised if everyone doesn't notice how great you are."

CHAPTER 7

◆◆◆◆◆

The Wedding Ring

AMA BILL PROTEST---RAILWAYS IN SHA

PRIVATE CANADIAN INTERESTS OPPOSE CANAL BILL

OTTAWA, Aug. 24.—It is stated here on the best authority that certain semi-public and great private Canadian interests are contemplating action in connection with the Panama bill, independent of representations, which may be made by Canada as a nation in conjunction with Great Britain. The bill as it stands at present involves a great many interests outside of the purely international phase of the question, and there is every reason to believe these interests are preparing for action apart from diplomatic representations.

HEAVY RAINFALL PUTS STOP TO THE MANITOBA HARVEST

Farmers in Eastern Manitoba Forced to Quit by Yesterday's Showers

WINNIPEG, Aug. 24.—Rain, steady and permanent in eastern Manitoba, and scattered showers further west, has tied up harvest operations for this week-end, but prospects are for higher temperatures and fair weather.

STATES CUSTOMS OFFICIAL AFTER GRAIN SMUGGLERS

George E. Foulkes to Come to Canada to Make an Investigation

MINNEAPOLIS, Minn., Aug. 24.—

DEFEAT
CIT
T

"Looks

MORE

Stampede cartoon in
Calgary Daily Herald, 1912
Glenbow Archives

A Couple of Runaways Meet

Soon enough Guy Weadick wanted everything about Flores LaDue. He wanted to knock the chip off her shoulder; he wanted to bury his face in her hair; he wanted to run the palm of his hand down the small of her back when she bent over to spin her figure eights.

He tried his usual and most successful forms of flirtation on her, with no success, so after a couple of weeks, he decided he'd have to adjust his methods. First he tried simply staring at her, in the hope of catching her glance, but she'd avert her eyes. He tried cornering her, but she proved far too elusive for that.

Flores LaDue was a pretty woman with a fine figure, and her curves were emphasized when she cinched her belt around her tiny waist. She also had magnificent chestnut brown hair, which she often wore tucked under her Stetson, revealing a delicate neck. Guy often found himself behind her, using all his might to resist touching that one lone strand of hair that escaped her hat and curled down her neck. But she always felt his presence. One day he paused behind her after practice as she was coiling lengths of rope over the horn of her saddle. Without turning around to face him, she said demurely, "Anything I can do for you, Mr. Weadick?"

"Teach me some fancy tricks," he said a little sheepishly, "and I'll try not to choke myself on my own rope."

Behind her, she heard the sound of her lariat spilling off the saddle's horn even though she had just tightly wrapped it. Things were coming apart—this was not a good sign. She was wary of Guy Weadick. He was just a little too smooth. She had seen him flirt with some of the other women in the show, and she knew more than a few of them who professed to be in love with him. She thought them fools and was determined that she would not be among them, so she kept her distance, and during their lessons, in the safety of the outdoors, she was a strict no-nonsense teacher.

"Okay," she said, "but you need to listen to me and do what I say. This is my job, Mr. Weadick, and I take it very seriously."

"All I can say is, I will try, but I find it very hard to concentrate around attractive women."

"Then I suggest that you spend more time with the cows and asses."

This was not going to be easy. Flores was proving to be a formidable challenge. He didn't know that she stole glances at him when he wasn't looking and that her hands shook a little when he entered the sawdust ring to work with her. He also didn't know that her nervousness around him made her ashamed of and annoyed with herself, which, in turn, made her even more prickly than usual.

"Well, now, Mr. Guy Weadick," she had said to him, "I heard some foolish girl say the other day that you could charm the birds out of the trees. But you need to know something—I sure as hell am no pigeon."

And yet, the more time they spent together, the more she struggled to fight her attraction. She loved the very tallness of him, the very handsomeness of him, and the very intelligence of him. But she didn't want to start relying on a man. After all, she had been on her own for a very long time, operating without a safety net to fall into, and she knew that she didn't have the option of running home to daddy at the first sign of trouble. Guy Weadick unnerved her, and the only time she felt she had any control of the situation was when she was in the ring teaching him how to rope. And that is the only place she agreed to meet him; he, of course, arranged to meet her every chance he got.

At one of their weekly sessions, she decided to let him practise with her prized lariat, made of six strips of rawhide braided together, that a Mexican vaquero had given her a few years before.

"These ropes were first used by the Spanish and Mexicans before grass ropes originated on the range," she said proudly as she handed him the lariat. She had expected and hoped that he would marvel at the craftsmanship of the leather or the beauty of the braiding, but he wasn't even looking at the rope that she so reverently placed in his big open hands. Instead, he stood there, looking at her. She suddenly felt like a gormless schoolgirl.

"All's I can say, Miss LaDue," he said, "is that you have the softest hands in the West."

From then on, she wore her gloves to their sessions. He noticed that she was always impeccably dressed, and her five-inch-long buckskin gloves with the flared gauntlets were now an added attraction. Flores LaDue got her gloves from an Indian woman who made them especially for her, and the more highly decorated with beadwork, fancy stitching, and fringe, the better. She also wore the gloves for protection from blisters, rope burns and, now, Guy Weadick's advances.

"Try again," she'd say, untangling a kink and passing the rope back into his hands. "Keep it dilated."

Though she was outwardly stingy with her praise, she had to admit that Guy was a quick study, and he was soon more than adept with a lariat. She admired this. And though he was slick, he was also joyful and reckless, qualities that she also admired. Still, her feelings changed from week to week. Could she see making a life with this charmer?

"I am not someone you can take lightly," she told him after twenty-one days of resisting his advances. But the first time he put his hand on her shoulder, she caved. They were standing together, and she was going on like a schoolmarm: "*Riata* is Spanish for rope. The North Americans shortened the word to *lariat*." At that point he moved toward her and said simply: "Who are you, Flores LaDue? Where did you come from?"

"I ran away from home," she said, and inexplicably began to cry.

"It's okay," he said, as he cupped her chin, "so did I."

The Runaways Fall in Love

By day twenty-eight, Guy and Flores had become a couple. Part of her wanted to keep the relationship secret—she'd been okay on her own for six years; she did not need a man to let her know who she was. Another part wanted to let everyone know that she was in love for the first time in her life, and she liked it. It was, therefore, almost a sign from above when the storm blew in. One afternoon, after exercising the horses, she ignored his offer to help with the grooming, Later she'd come upon him alone, sitting cross-legged against the barn, waiting for her.

"There is something not right. It is too quiet," he said, closing his eyes against the sun. "It's too hot and too quiet."

And sure enough, the air was hot and heavy. She removed her Stetson and waved it in front of her face as she scanned the sideshow tents. Suddenly out of the corner of her eye, she saw the tents start to billow and the ropes holding the pegs to flap. Within seconds, a violent wind full of sand began to blow in. Guy jumped up and grabbed her hand, but the wind pushed them back against the building. He pulled her hand hard, and they ran along the side of the barn as hailstones pelted them. "In here," he yelled, yanking her inside and pushing the door shut. She gasped for breath; he emptied the brim of his Stetson of hailstones and wiped his face with the back of his hand.

"This is shapin' up to be a pretty good day," he said, smiling like a cat in a creamery. "At last I have you behind closed doors."

He gripped her shoulders, turned her around, and, though it had taken him four weeks to get it there, he put his hand in the small of her back to guide her toward two hay bales in the middle of the floor. He sat her down on one, and he sat down facing her on the other. He moved her knees together inside his and under the relentless pounding of hailstones above them, he began his sales pitch.

"You ever heard of the Calgary Exhibition?" he asked. "It's been held every summer since 1886 up in Alberta, Canada."

She said that she'd only been to a place called Winnipeg in what she believed was a province called Manitoba.

"I can't get Alberta out of my system," he said, "and Calgary either. You have to see this place. It is still the Wild West. And I hear it's the fastest growing city in Alberta. The Canadian Pacific Railway goes there and folks are moving in from everywhere."

All she could hear was the howling of the wind. What was going on here? The storm had brought them together, they were soaking wet and stranded in a barn, and all he could talk about was some place in Canada that she had barely heard of.

He went on: "I know about this because I was promoting Will Pickett at the 1904 Calgary Exhibition, and up there they got snake-oil salesmen, a circus, agricultural and grain exhibits, farm animals, clothing, furniture and brewery merchants, cooking, handicrafts, horse and stagecoach races. Plumb near everything but a rodeo." His big hands, now with both thumbs on either side of her inseam, had released their grip on her knees and moved halfway up the material of her split skirt. Was he toying with her?

"They've been having that Exhibition up there for twenty years, and it's just sitting there waiting for me to add a rodeo to it, Florence," he said. He needed his own name for her. "But the political and financial dynamics aren't right in Calgary just yet, so I want to offer you something else in the meantime."

She didn't move. "Such as?"

He stood up now. "It seems like a natural progression that Will Pickett, you, and I go it alone to Broadway, and a tour of Europe with Buffalo Bill's Wild West Show. I've been working on this behind the scenes, so I know they want all three of us."

She was furious.

"You upset about something?" he asked innocently.

"You think you can come here and turn my life upside down like this. You make plans for my life without even talking to me first!? Do you expect me to throw everything overboard and ride into another life with you like some kind of circus pony?"

He paused and smiled, then walked toward a saddle resting on a wall peg, a coil of rope hanging on its rope strap. He un-coiled the rope, walked to the centre of the barn, and turned, looking straight at her. She looked straight back. With agile fin-

Florence & Guy Weadick, circa 1927

McLean family collection

gers he made a loop with the rope. "Come here," he said, and it was not a suggestion.

Almost despite herself, she approached him. He grasped her left shoulder and pulled her toward him before gently pushing her into a half turn away from him. She pressed against him, sinking back into the cast of his body.

"Feel, don't think," he said, and tilted her chin skyward. "Watch this." He gathered the rope and released it to whirl three times about their heads. Then he lofted the loop high up into the canopied beams of the roof. Through the rope's orbit, Flores LaDue saw a barn swallow dip its wings, as if in slow motion. She was intensely aware of Guy, the smell of him, his circular movements against her body.

As the rope fell, it spread in a large circle that lassoed both of them.

"I know you never cast it," he said to her, "but this trick's called the Wedding Ring. So, Miss Flores LaDue, what say we go on down to Memphis and get married?"

CHAPTER 8

◆◆◆◆◆

A Seed Is Planted

Dominion Exhibition
poster, 1908

Glenbow Archives NA-1473-1

The 1908 Dominion Exhibition, Calgary, Alberta

Flores LaDue, twenty-three, and Guy Weadick, twenty-one, were married in Memphis, Tennessee, on November 17, 1906. At the time of their marriage, they had known each other for exactly five weeks.

After their wedding, the Weadicks saw a lot of country. Billed alternately as Weadick & LaDue, Stampede Riders, or Wild West Stunts, they took their dog and roping act across North America on the small-time circuit of travelling circuses, rodeos, and Wild West shows. But the perfect training ground for them was the impressive, long-running Miller Brothers 101 Ranch and Real Wild West Show, out of Oklahoma, that eventually signed them. There they crossed paths with the most famous stars of the vaudeville circuit, and they morphed into rapid adapters who could spin yarns with show-biz celebrities, fast pack a trunk for the next train stop, add comic relief to three performances a day, and tailor their act to any stage.

In 1908, the Miller Brothers show was appearing at Madison Square Garden, in New York City. After a successful run there, the show packed up and joined a forty-five-railroad-car touring contingent bound for the Great Dominion Exhibition in western Canada. Calgary, to be specific. The Exhibition was an annual event that travelled from city to city, showcasing regional diversity; it was generously subsidized with $50,000 from the Canadian federal government.

The gospel of growth was being sung loud and strong in Calgary. The population stood at 25,000, and the potential seemed unlimited; word on the street was that by the next decade the population of this shining star of the West would reach 100,000. Despite the worst winter on record for cattle ranchers, others, including civic boosters, real estate developers, financial advisors, the *Calgary Daily Herald*, and the boards of trade, Calgary was riding a wave of prosperity, fuelled mostly by speculation and wild imaginations.

The Weadicks arrived in Calgary in early July of 1908, and Florence Weadick was immediately impressed. She loved the cool crisp air, delivered courtesy of winds over the Rockies, and the many attractive sandstone buildings; she would learn about Calgary's great fire of 1886, which had burned many wooden-framed structures in the city to the ground. Ever since then, the city had not allowed wooden buildings, insisting instead that contractors mine the many sandstone quarries outside the city for fireproof material. By the 1890s, half of Calgary's tradesmen were stonemasons, and the city was often called the Sandstone City. Not only would the new Grain Exchange Building be made of sandstone, it would be the tallest building in the city. To Florence's eyes, though, the white-capped mountains off to the west already rimmed the city like a giant metropolis. She was also impressed by the Exhibition grounds, where a king's ransom of provincial and city funding ($35,000 and $25,000, respectively), had made possible the erection of new handicraft and livestock exhibit buildings, a roofed grandstand, and a half-dozen new stables.

The 1908 Exhibition was a huge success, and attendance was estimated at about 100,000 over seven days, despite terrible weather and an economic depression. People came from across the four western Canadian provinces and also from the United States—indeed, many Americans from as far away as Spokane, Washington, came on special rail cars to celebrate the American national holiday, July 4, in a place that was still seen as the authentic Old West.

The Exhibition offered some unique attractions, one of which was a propeller-driven hydrogen balloon called Strobel's airship, which made a number of successful flights over Victoria Park, the main ground of the Exhibition. Unfortunately, a strong gust of wind blew the airship against the grandstand building and it burst into flames; fortunately, no one was killed.

That aside, the Exhibition was a feast of colour and music, with dozens of marching bands and floats from many different ethnic groups that contributed to its great success. Because it was essentially an agricultural and rural celebration, at least 2,500 animals were entered into judged competitions, and major agricultural exhibits stood alongside industrial ones. The event also featured an all-female band, acrobats, a wild animal circus, and vaudeville entertainers. The Western theme honouring ranch life was quite evident: the midway was called the Roundup, and the exhibits were displayed in an area known as the Corral. During Western Day, Indians raced horses, and cowboys competed for prizes. Dignitaries in attendance in-

cluded Senator James Lougheed and the first lieutenant governor of Alberta, George Bulyea.

And to really emphasize the Western theme, the Miller
Brothers 101 Ranch and Real Wild West Show was on hand to
stage three shows in one day, all under its own canvas tent. No
Miller performance garnered more applause than the Weadicks'
witty and original trick roping act, which was billed as "Roping and Gab." The couple won over every audience with their
perfectly matched talents—Flores, with her almost sensual skill
with a lariat, and Guy, with his charisma and amusing dialogue,
in which he assured the audience that any one of them could
learn to do what he and Florence were doing.

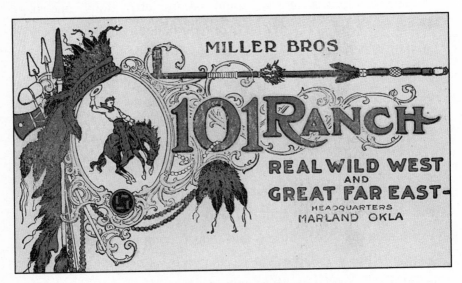

Miller Brothers 101 Ranch postcard

McLean family collection

"The toughest trick is the Butterfly," Guy would say.
"You start it like this . . ." The rope would go into a knot.
"So you start again like this . . ." Another knot appeared.

"So you start again and try to reverse like this . . ." Another knot.

"In fact," he would wind up, "the durned thing is so tough it's impossible," whereupon, as if by magic, the loop would start doing figure eights in a perfect butterfly.

Something else occurred as if by magic during that week in Calgary in 1908. A seed of an idea was planted in Guy Weadick's brain. He could clearly see Calgary's potential as a staging ground for a Wild West show to end all Wild West shows. It had a growing population, it was right in the middle of true Western country, and it had cowboys and ranchers and colourful characters galore. And most important, it had spirit.

CHAPTER 9

◆◆◆◆◆

Fair Weather and Funds

The Dominion Exhibition of 1908 came to an end. Down at the grounds, exhausted day labourers lined up at the payroll window. The wind kicked up and blew used tickets, torn programs, and tumbleweed across the racetrack. Cowboys shipped out, ranchers trailed 675 head of cattle and over 600 horses out of the city, farm families from the four western provinces dismantled over forty agricultural displays, and the last semblance of vaudeville impresarios prepared to leave for their next gig.

On that last night, a few rodeo stragglers gathered for the larded moose rump roast that was served for Sunday dinner at the Alberta Hotel restaurant. Before dinner, Florence and the ladies made themselves comfortable in the hotel rotunda on the deep-buttoned leather chesterfields stuffed with horsehair. They were waiting for their men, who stood at the hotel bar, the longest in western Canada, quaffing beer and whisky, before repairing to the restaurant—women did not go into the bar, with the exception of the notorious Caroline "Mother" Fulham, who was said to be able to match any man drink for drink. During the week of the Exhibition, though, Florence had stood at the bar with her husband, and she didn't give a damn who saw her. But this was Sunday, and Florence knew that when families with children were in attendance, the bar was no place for a woman.

Later, over a quiet supper together, she listened while her vaudeville showman husband talked endlessly about the Exhibition. When Calgary had been awarded the 1908 Exhibition, manager Ernie Richardson, an inspired and able administrator, had barely had a year to organize it, but he had done a bang-on job, and the Exhibition had been a resounding success.

"Ernie organized that whole damn Exhibition in less than a year. Imagine that. He had to contact all those people, get the Native groups on his side, find hotel rooms or billets for everybody. You know they set up beds in empty schools to deal with all those tourists? And he had to advertise it all, too. Let all interested folks from Winnipeg to Vancouver, from Montana to Minnesota, know about it."

"Well, he sure did a great job, don't you think?"

"I do. And what is even more, he made money. And I figure we could, too."

"Don't stop talking now."

"Flo, I figure that a real Western show is what this city needs. Look at it. I can feel it. I figure that first-class afternoon and evening performances could fill the grandstand every single day. I reckon an event like that—done proper—could turn a profit of, I don't know, twenty, twenty-five thousand."

Florence admired and shared her husband's enthusiasm, but other thoughts were going through her mind. Her memory strayed back to the minute she stepped off the train and fell in love with Calgary. She figured that this city, in the middle of a huge expanse of prairie and infused with a love of Western culture, could be a home for them. Here was the perfect mixture of

American, Canadian, European, and Native peoples, a ranching history, a grain-farming industry, and a major exhibition already in place. And she and Guy had reached the crux of their rodeo careers—maybe it was time to think about settling somewhere.

"What do you think, Florence?"

"What?"

"What do you think?"

"Sorry. I drifted off. But I hear what you are saying. You want to know what I think? I think that you and I are the best rodeo entertainers that the Wild West circuits have ever produced." She paused. "And if we got permanent funding for your dream, we could cut a swath through this town like a wagon wheel through a wheat field."

His wife's words electrified him. This had been his dream for years, but he realized that if he took too long to act on it, somebody else could come along and beat him to the punch. "Back in Iowa, I told you my idea of a rodeo was a perfect fit with the Inter-Western Pacific Exhibition Company. I've just got to figure out how to bring it all together. You saw how good we dovetailed with the Dominion."

"It was damn good. So what do we have to do to make this a reality?"

"Well, I am not too sure about that yet."

Florence was intensely loyal to her husband, but when he dithered, she could be a brutal critic, and she could swear a blue streak if she had to. She thought she had to. As she leaned forward to speak, nearby conversations ground to a halt. "Well, you better figure it out pretty damned soon," she chastised him. "We need money to pull this thing off. Your job is to find it."

And that's when Guy Weadick knew what he had to do next.

The next day, he reacquainted himself with H. C. McMullen, the livestock agent for the Canadian Pacific Railway. Back in the late 1870s, McMullen had trailed some of the first cattle across the border from Montana into the North-West Territories, and when he arrived in what would eventually become Alberta, he liked it so much that he never left. A leathery old cowpoke who was known to ease his equestrian-related aches with the odd whisky at the Alberta Hotel bar, McMullen was a popular figure in Calgary. Guy Weadick had been immediately drawn to him when they met in Calgary several years before at the 1905 Exhibition and discovered that they had many mutual friends. During the previous week in Calgary, the lounges had been full of entrepreneurs cooking up the next big thing for rodeo, and Guy Weadick had shot the breeze with most of them. Everyone, that is, except H. C. McMullen. Now, with Weadick's ears still burning with his wife's fiery words, he made an appointment.

People said that it took a lot of effrontery on Guy Weadick's part to approach the well-known livestock agent, and Weadick would be the first one to agree with them. But effrontery he had in spades. And it paid off. There was something about the young brash extrovert that H. C. McMullen liked—Weadick clearly had a sense of showmanship and was smart to boot. After a few rounds, the ringmaster and the livestock agent parted with a friendly handshake and a promise to keep in touch to discuss their favourite topic: Calgary as the perfect location to establish a big-scale cowboy championship and reunion of Western pioneers. They also agreed that if they could ever organize such an event with the cream of rodeo, their biggest enemy would be the weather, and their biggest challenge would be raising money.

CHAPTER 10

◆◆◆◆◆

Travels on the Continent

The world seemed to overflow with possibilities for Florence and Guy Weadick in 1908 as they made their way south to Medicine Hat for the Alberta provincial riding and roping championships. Guy was especially pleased to see a large contingent of Blood Indians pack the bleachers, including Crop Eared Wolf, who cut a curious figure wearing the leggings and moccasins of the Indian and a white man's jacket with a button bearing Guy's photo on the lapel.

Florence knew that in Alberta she had finally found her spot on earth, although it turned out that she was not going to settle there quite yet. Soon, she and Guy boarded a puffing steam train bound for Broadway, where they awed audiences in a vaudeville production entitled *Billy the Kid*. After this, they headed south to Jacksonville, Florida, where they enjoyed the warmth of the Florida winter and turned down their first offer to star in a series of Western moving pictures. It was an easy decision for them—the movie industry was in its infancy, and Florence and Guy Weadick loved nothing more than performing in front of a live audience.

If postcards could talk, the collection of them from Florence and Guy's years on the road between 1908 and 1911 would tell some fascinating stories. The vintage stamps and dates on the cards show that they crossed the continent during those years, putting on shows in California, Colorado, Connecticut, Idaho, Illinois, Ohio, Oregon, Louisiana, New York, and Vermont. They also returned north to Canada, for the rodeo in Morris, Manitoba. Yet they never received another invitation to go back to Calgary, even though that city was going through one of its famous booms—the population had doubled to 50,000.

And so it was that, on February 23, 1911, Florence and Guy Weadick walked their horses up the gangplank of the SS *Laurentic* and set sail for Liverpool, England, as part of the Miller Brothers' 101 Ranch and Real Wild West Show. Accompanying them in the noise and confusion on the dock were Guy's brother Tom, Bill Sellman (nicknamed Bridle Bill), five trick ponies, and a little Boston bull terrier named Bum. The stupendous tricks that Bum performed brought in half the money Florence and Guy would need to purchase their Stampede Ranch a decade later. When Bum died, the Weadicks had him stuffed and mounted in a place of honour near their fireplace, where the sight of him would later give many a guest a fright. But Florence was adamant about keeping him there: "It's a fitting tribute to a loyal pal who helped pay for this ranch," she would say. As they began their European tour, no thought of a ranch in Alberta or anywhere else entered their heads. Instead the question was: How long would it be before they could settle down anywhere?

They opened their European tour in Glasgow and booked in with Buffalo Bill's Wild West Show, which was also touring Scotland. The appetite for all things from the American West had been whetted by the fabulous stories told by the families of the many Scots who had emigrated, by articles in newspapers and magazines, and, of course, by the astounding feats of the performers in the Wild West shows. Audiences couldn't get enough of them, and Florence was gratified to pull in big crowds wherever they went, though one thing that had come to annoy her was the portrayal of Indians in the shows. In one act, a weather-beaten wagon would slowly make its way across the arena, women and children and strong boxes full of valuables inside. Suddenly a group of war-painted Indians on horseback, yelling at the top of their lungs, would swoop down and set fire to the cloth covering of the wagon. The petrified passengers would flee the vehicle amid smoke and the sound of fake bullets and the horrible sight of Indians "scalping" defenceless innocents by seeming to cut off their hair. This staged gun battle left the Scots breathless with admiration at the bravery of the settlers who faced the bloodthirsty and treacherous Indians; it left both Florence and Guy with a bad taste in their mouths. Florence couldn't help but think back to the time when she was known as Grace Maud Bensel and spent the best years of her life with the Sioux, who she knew to be honourable and brave people. The Sioux, and lots of other Indians, too, had been dealt a raw deal by the white man on both sides of the forty-ninth parallel. But she knew enough to pick her battles wisely, so she managed to control herself during this time, especially in London, when Lord Lonsdale, a horseman and aristocrat of the old school who was taken with the Miller Brothers' 101 Ranch Real Wild West Show, became friendly with them. He'd examined with interest their horses, saddlery, and dress, and finally asked them how he could make their stay in London memorable. No one tells the story better than Guy Weadick's neighbour Raymond Patterson, who first heard it in front of the fireplace in the long room of the Stampede Ranch and later published it in his book *Far Pastures*.

Yes, Guy Weadick said, there was. If it were possible, they would enjoy most of all seeing over Buckingham Palace stables—horses, harnesses, carriages, everything.

Very well, Lord Lonsdale replied: he thought that could be arranged. There was just one thing, he continued—and one may suppose there was a smile on his face as he spoke. He wanted them to come on horseback, in full war-paint—chaps, boots, sombreros, fringed and beaded gloves and jackets—everything just as in the show. Let them assemble at ten o'clock the next morning at Prince's Gate in Hyde Park—but casually; not in a body, but in twos and threes as if they were out for a morning ride.

And so it was arranged.

The next morning the twos and threes, bright as butterflies against the quiet London scene, riding in Rotten Row [the name of a track running along the south side of Hyde Park. Even today it serves as a place to ride horses in the centre of London.] began to attract attention. Occasionally they stopped to greet each other, and small, admiring crowds assembled. The crowds grew and followed the cowboys. The police intervened and said that the riders could not be allowed to create a disturbance, riding around in fancy dress. The Americans, all innocence, said it wasn't fancy dress—it was just their ordinary working clothes, all they had to ride in, and they had always wanted to ride in Rotten Row. A highlight of their English visit. The police were baffled; and slowly, and with perfect timing, the 101 Ranch closed in on Prince's Gate, just where the motor road cuts across between Hyde Park and Kensington Gardens.

A glorious traffic jam was the immediate result. Buses were stopped, the old open-top buses, and people swarmed up on top of them to cheer and laugh. The London crowd took charge, always unpredictable, this time delighted. Carriages, cars, taxis, riders in sober black or grey, nursemaids with perambulators—everything came to a standstill. It was a good-natured riot.

Precisely on the stroke of ten Lord Lonsdale appeared. He was probably one of the best-known and most popular men in London at that time. The crowd roared its welcome; and soon, by the magic of his smile, his lordship had everybody soothed—police, bus-drivers, taxi-drivers, even, let us hope, the orthodox, bowler-hatted riders and those who, by now, had quite certainly missed their trains. Soon, with Guy Weadick and the other top men of the 101 Ranch, he was riding easily towards Buckingham Palace—the whole gorgeous cavalcade following behind him, guests, for the morning, of the King.

Flores LaDue knew that when her time came, she would depict Indians in a positive light, but for now, if her husband decided that it took cowboys and Indians to get attention in England, then so be it. At the very least, the British audiences understood horsemanship. The depiction of the Wild West was a new experience to tens of thousands of Londoners, who watched them at the Palladium, an area of London known as White City, the Leicester Square Empire, the Crystal Palace, and the Alhambra Theatre. In Germany, for her star turn at the Wintergarten, in Berlin, she stood on a saddle on a horse that galloped around the arena at a breakneck pace. In St. Petersburg and Moscow, Florence Weadick proved to Russian audiences that a cowgirl could be as proficient as a cowboy, when she caught and roped runaway horses at top speed. In Vienna she would enter the arch of the arena lying flat on her horse's back, then sit astride her horse, tossing twists and loops of her lariat, as it cantered around the infield.

But it was in Paris that the Weadicks felt most energized. Perhaps it was the latitude—at 48 degrees north, Paris is on almost the same latitude as Calgary, at 51. Or perhaps it was the atmosphere; Paris seemed made for youth, beauty, and pleasure. And fashion, of course. Indeed, Florence Weadick must have cut an amazing figure and displayed a new form of femininity in her loose, long-sleeved shirt, flat boots, wide-brimmed Stetson, and an engraved gold belt that encircled the tiny waist of her divided skirt. But that wasn't the only show Guy and Florence put on in Paris; Parisians sipping espresso in fashionable cafés might have thought they were people of the world who had seen everything, but they never imagined that they would ever see a horse on the Eiffel Tower. But when Guy Weadick decreed that he would take his horse up the famous Paris landmark, so many people bet that he wouldn't do it, that he did. Indeed, Guy ruffled even more French feathers when he almost got involved in a duel to the death. Again, the story is best told by Raymond Patterson:

Guy Weadick in Paris, 1911

Museum of the Highwood

It was on a spring evening in Paris, during that same visit, that Guy, headed for the theatre, stopped somewhere on the Boulevard des Italiens for a shave and a shampoo. He was grossly overcharged, but had not sufficient French to argue about it. Also, he was late, so he paid and got out. However, he took it out on the barber during the act, ad-libbing to his heart's content before an audience that was largely English and American. They loved it, and it went so well that Guy slipped it into the act from that night onwards. But the French had evidently appreciated it also, for a voluble little delegation called round at Guy's dressing-room, on that first night, to tell him so. He could understand that much because the word "satisfaction" kept cropping up, again and again. He bowed and smiled and said, with appropriate gestures, that he was indeed happy to know that they had enjoyed the act. But they went on and on about it; and finally, in desperation, Guy got hold of a French theatre attendant who could speak a little English. "Tell these guys," he said, "that I'm pleased they enjoyed the show. And get them the hell out of here—I want to change and go."

It was only then that it became clear that these Frenchmen had not enjoyed the act at all. They were the friends of the barber, who had been in the house when Guy was saying his piece about the highway robbers of the Boulevard des Italiens—worse, he had said, than any of the holdup men who had once shot it out in the wild days of the American frontier. The barber's honour had been affronted and the satisfaction his friends were talking about was a duel to the death.

As the challenged party, Guy had the choice of weapons. He promptly suggested the lariat; or, if the barber preferred it, he volunteered to knock him into the middle of next week at any given spot in the Forêt de Whatsitsname (and let the barber name it) the very next morning. Uproar broke loose at this ungentlemanly suggestion, and finally Guy shooed the whole lot out, changed out of his Western finery and went his way.

Though Guy made some blustery noises about accepting the challenge, Florence's cooler head prevailed. It was time to head back to Canada—a letter from Calgary had just reached them: H. C. McMullen had written and implored them to return. He had some interesting information for them. It was just as well; Guy Weadick was never going to be a cowboy who ate quiche.

—CHAPTER II—

◆◆◆◆◆

The Seed Germinates

Upon their return to Calgary, McMullen invited the Weadicks to the Exhibition grounds, and as they walked, he gave them a crash course in the city's history. Calgary's first Exhibition was prompted by an August 6, 1884, suggestion by Thomas Braden, an editor with the *Calgary Daily Herald*, who made a challenge that no self-respecting Calgarian could refuse. In order to stop Ontario from bad-mouthing the West, Braden wrote from the tent city on the banks of the Bow River, Albertans should organize an exhibition to display the agricultural wealth of the province, then everything should be loaded onto a CPR express car and sent to tour the farming districts of Ontario.

McMullen also told the Weadicks about Major James Walker, another popular Albertan. Walker had graduated from the Royal Military College in Kingston, Ontario, and entered the ranks of the North-West Mounted Police, where he became an inspector, a major, and, finally, a colonel. Walker endured the hardships of the march west and served with distinction at several forts, including Fort Walsh and Fort Calgary. Upon his retirement in 1881, he accepted the position of local manager of the Cochrane Ranch, and two years later went into the lumber business. He purchased a large sawmill, and when the CPR arrived in 1883 he was perfectly positioned to supply the timber for its bridges and railroad ties.

Alberta's land boom attracted immigrants from Eastern Europe, Asia, Great Britain, Ireland, and the United States, and the government was faced with the task of uniting farmers, ranchers, trades, and professional people as Albertans. Agriculture would give them the means to do so.

Calgary's first agricultural Exhibition was held October 19–20, 1886, at the Star skating rink and the surrounding patch of treeless bald prairie. Prizes were awarded for the best livestock, grains, produce, flowers, and handicrafts. Over 500 people attended the harvest fair over the two days. New homesteaders were introduced to the realities of Alberta's capricious climate when a blizzard arrived the day before the fair opened and blocked some of the outlying trails into the city. Nevertheless, snow did not diminish James Walker's enthusiasm for the Exhibition, and he joined his fellow citizens in rounding up support and raising money for the next year. But what set Walker apart was that he never missed an opportunity. In fact, two years earlier, Walker had capitalized on an idea that would secure the land for the future Stampede. It was 1884, and Walker was on an inspection tour of the federal experimental farm southwest of the city, at Fish Creek, with A. M. Burgess, then minister of the interior and deputy minister of agriculture. Burgess fell off his horse and broke his collarbone, and Walker took him into his home for treatment while the injury healed. Halfway through the healing process, Walker took Burgess on a walking tour of the present site of Stampede Park. During their walk, they stopped directly across from the steep walls of the cut bank that descended into a natural amphitheatre circling the Elbow River

Valley from north to south. The hillside excluded their north/ south view, but the site had obvious advantages: to the west a plateau overlooked a ninety-six-acre parcel of open plain surrounded by a wide bend of the meandering river. Beyond lay the majestic Rocky Mountains.

Walker proposed organizing an annual exhibition and fair at the spot that would incorporate a racetrack, cattle sheds, and agricultural buildings, and he asked Burgess if the federal government would support the sale of this land to the Calgary Exhibition. Burgess said that it might, if the organization proved viable. Unfortunately, it didn't. The great fire of 1886 and the harsh winter of 1886–87, when cattle ranchers suffered huge winter losses, made for dismal attendance at the agricultural fair. The following year entries in the various categories again fell short, and members of the Exhibition board knew they had to increase the pressure on the federal government to sell the land. The alternative was to dump the fair altogether.

After the Exhibition's request for financial assistance from the federal government, I. S. G. Van Wart, a transplanted Torontonian who had Liberal Party connections in Ottawa, added some political muscle and, in the end, the federal government sold the property to the committee for $2.50 an acre, and the Exhibition, at last, had some land and seed money.

This, then, was the situation that faced Florence and Guy Weadick in March of 1912.

"Just to set you straight," McMullen said as they walked by the cattle sheds, "I don't have much time for federal governments, but one of the smartest things those boys in Ottawa did was put a caveat on the land that it was never to be sold or subdivided, and any attempt to do so would result in the government repossessing all ninety-four acres. And once the deed was registered in 1889," McMullen continued, "the board of the society couldn't wait for the ink to dry so they could mortgage the property for three thousand dollars and start building."

Since then the grounds had been known as Victoria Park, and the Exhibition grew with all kinds of year-long activities, such as livestock shows, exhibitions of all kinds, horse auctions, and specialty stock shows, to name a few.

"Course the newspaper supported the Exhibition because their editor had suggested it in the first place," chuckled Mc-Mullen, "and by the turn of the century, veterinarian and cattleman Alexander Cross talked a few others into taking the fair to another level." They were now walking through the bullpens, and Weadick broke off midsentence, pointed to a big bull, and said: "If that bull had side pockets, he'd be packin' a pistol." Florence booted her husband in the shins, something that she did quite often.

"Well, it wouldn't be the first pistol in Calgary," McMullen said, and smiled, adding in a more serious tone, "but with expanding the Exhibition we can move forward to draw the ranchers together with all the new citizens of this fair city—farmers, tradesmen, and professional people—to gather for a single purpose: to all get better acquainted and celebrate the manifestations of our achievements in the West."

"Now that's what I call an endorsement," replied Weadick, glad-handing McMullen. "Now we just have to find someone to finance it."

Guy Weadick had been around exhibitions for a long time and knew that at the turn of the century A. E. Cross had formed the nonprofit Inter-Western Pacific Exhibition Company with the idea of staging the biggest midsummer exhibition between Winnipeg and the West Coast. He mentioned this to McMullen.

"That was the hell of it," continued McMullen, "because right then the Exhibition board fell on hard times, the mortgage was foreclosed, and R. B. Bennett held the title to Victoria Park."

As they strolled by the roofed grandstand, McMullen told them that Walker had shown Burgess a postcard photograph of the CPR special car that went across Canada in 1884, stuffed full with Alberta's bounty.

"Agricultural Society Secretary J. G. Fitzgerald accompanied this car, and when those Easterners saw stalks of Alberta wheat six feet long, they accused him of splicing the two stalks together," snorted McMullen. "Walker once told me that the Easterners figured Albertans were just snot-nosed pretenders from the wrong side of the country, but he said that that express car gave the prairies a start to display its harvest."

That said, the fact was that Calgary City Council had provided grants to offset the fair's $7,000 deficit. "A. E. Cross was an honourable man and he had a slow fuse; he never let emotion get in the way of reason," continued McMullen. Cross persuaded Bennett to give them a one-year lease, and the 1899 Exhibition showed a small profit. McMullen went on, "By 1901, Cross and his associates had persuaded the city to buy the acreage from Bennett and lease it to the company. By 1904 the Exhibition was firmly entrenched as an annual event, and the campaign to get the 1908 Dominion Exhibition for Calgary had already begun when I first saw you. As I recall, you were making quite a bit of noise that day."

McMullen was right—he had first seen Guy Weadick standing in the infield using a megaphone to blare out the news of Bill Pickett's bulldogging act at the 1905 Calgary Exhibition. Guy was now thoughtfully patrolling the fence along the infield.

"That act had bankability," Guy said. "After the Exhibition here, Bill and I headed down to Chicago, where I first saw Florence," he said, putting an arm around his wife. "Luckiest day of my life. We came back to perform here in 1908 when Calgary hosted the Dominion Exhibition, and that parade set a good tone. It's just too damn bad Calgary couldn't keep getting that federal, provincial, and city money you got for the Dominion because then things wouldn't o' got slowed down like they are now."

"The emblems of civilization in our midst today—the railroad, fences, and the automobile—have darn near ruined this annual exhibition," McMullen sighed. "Did you know that people are starting to drive those gasoline buggies up to Banff?"

It was all true. Old-timers were passing away, the days of the open range were ending, and the story of the cowboy risked being consigned to a kind of mythical past. Calgary's growth had been slow but steady since 1905, and by 1909, the population stood at 29,265. Then in the boom years between 1909 and 1912, the population skyrocketed to almost 80,000—the city streets teemed with industrialists and bankers and businessmen who wanted the city to shed its frontier image.

But there were many who were dedicated to keeping the Western sensibility alive and to promoting the rodeo as the quintessential Western event—people like Ad Day, owner of the Big Horse Ranch, south of Medicine Hat. Day owned a string of bucking horses and staged small local competitions featuring Wild West performers like Tom Mix, referred to by some as Hollywood's first Western megastar. Mix suggested that Day get to Calgary to talk big rodeo with McMullen. Inspired by the idea of a huge event in Calgary, Day told McMullen he'd put up $10,000 in cash and supply his best horses and stock if Guy Weadick could get more financial sponsorship.

"Another Day, another dollar," McMullen had deadpanned to himself as he dropped that fateful letter to Guy Weadick in Paris into the postbox and banged the lid shut. Now that they were both in Calgary, they could pursue their common goal.

"You two have to be the ones to take the decision," said Florence Weadick matter-of-factly to her husband and McMullen as they paused in front of the empty grandstand. The day had been overcast, but now the sun was out. Florence held her hand to her eyes and squinted up at the two conspirators. She had every faith in their abilities, and what's more, she shared their ambitions.

McMullen smiled wide. His plan, which had been a germ of an idea only months before, was going to work. He could feel it. And so could Guy Weadick.

CHAPTER 12

◆◆◆◆◆

George Lane Appears on the Scene

Stampede grounds, circa 1908

Glenbow Archives NA-2913-6 and NA-3752-25

After a particularly intense yarning session, Guy Weadick and H. C. McMullen produced a document that they would shop around to the Calgary business community to raise money. Their proposal was to hold a week-long celebration of the pioneers, cowboys, and ranchers who had settled the West. Its official name was "Frontier Days and Cowboy Championship Contest," but to distinguish it from other rodeos, roundups, and frontier days, they would call it the "Stampede."

They had all sorts of grand ideas for what the Stampede could be. There was just one thing they didn't have—the $100,000 they needed to get started.

Guy's idea for getting around this slight financial setback was to approach Ernie Richardson, who had almost single-handedly organized the 1908 Dominion Exhibition in under a year. He knew that Richardson liked him and thought well of him, or he believed that he did, but when Guy approached Richardson with his fabulous idea, the latter balked. He was not impressed with Guy's financial proposal and was dismayed that he wanted to use the Calgary Industrial Exhibition's facilities. Both he and the president of the board of directors, I. S. G. Van Wart, figured that Weadick's and McMullen's "Frontier Days and

Cowboy Championship Contest" sounded like a hare-brained scheme. He had to hand it to Guy Weadick, though. The man had nerve.

"Not going to happen," Ernie Richardson had said flatly. "We don't want any cowboys around here; this city is growing."

"Well, every man has a right to his own opinions," said McMullen as he and Weadick left Richardson's office. "We'll just bypass him because there are better pickin's than that teetotalling tightwad."

Florence and Guy were having a coffee in the Alberta Hotel the next morning when Aleck Fleming, manager of the enormous Bar U Ranch, approached them. It seemed that his boss, George Lane, had heard about the idea for Frontier Days and wanted to learn more. Not only was Lane wealthy, he was a true ranchman, a man of substance who loved and appreciated the cowboy mythology. Born into a Quaker family, Lane became a United States cavalry scout and dispatch rider, and cowpunched on some of the biggest and most famous ranches in Montana before heading north to Alberta in 1884. Two years prior to that, in 1882, an Alberta stockman by the name of Fred Stimson had urged Montreal investors to found the North-West Cattle Company near Longview, Alberta. This massive ranch would eventually be known far and wide as the Bar U. By 1889 George Lane had been hired as the hardworking foreman at the Bar U; by 1902 he was the principal owner.

Lane provided a contrast to the growing population of businessmen in Calgary, who wore suits to work and sat behind desks. He was the real deal—a tough cowboy who shunned the limelight but was never too shy to fight for what he believed in. And he believed in the value of traditional Western culture. A dour man with thick eyebrows and a big handlebar moustache, Lane had the best glower in town and treated most city people with brusque indifference.

Guy Weadick hoped that in Lane he had found someone to help him realize his dream, and with a do-or-die attitude he went to meet him in his room at the Alberta Hotel. Guy made his pitch, described his vision, then asked for a stupendous amount of money. He was encouraged when Lane did not laugh him out of the room. In fact, to Guy's surprise, Lane told him to return later that afternoon to meet three of his friends to discuss the matter further. Lane had been impressed by Weadick; he thought his idea for a so-called Stampede was interesting. But more than that, he thought that such an event would help preserve the story of Alberta's ranchers, cowboys, and cattle industry before they slipped into history.

Guy left to find Florence outside waiting for him in front of the hotel by one of the few hitching posts that had not given way to automobiles. He was excited but nervous. How well had the meeting really gone? Had he been too bold, too flippant? What did George Lane really think? Only Florence knew this insecure side of hell-raiser Guy Weadick, who always seemed so cocky and self-assured. As a comfort, she linked her arm with his, and they turned east to walk down Atlantic Avenue toward the Exhibition grounds. In their Western clothing, he and Florence aroused some curious looks; the city was changing and more men were wearing fedoras and suits than Stetsons and Western wear, and Flores's split skirts and beautiful cowboy boots contrasted sharply with the prevailing ladies' fashion of the day: floor-length flowing skirts, large elaborate hats, and umbrellas to protect delicate skin from the sun. And it wasn't only fashion that was changing: streetcars clanged past them on paved streets where horses had once kicked up dust.

After considerable silence Guy said hesitantly, "I'd be shamed-up pretty good if George Lane turns me down."

"You have to promote yourself, Guy, because no one else is going to."

They stopped for lunch at a restaurant down by the streetcar barns at Victoria Park, then made their way back to the corner of First Street West, passing through pasturages green with cultivated grass. Now they were about to part. Little did either know that they were about to become members of a cast that included the most prestigious men in Calgary: ringmaster George Lane, ranchers Alfred Ernest Cross and Patrick Burns, and a necessary evil in the form of a politician named Archie McLean, a provincial secretary in the Alberta government at the time, who would come into the mix later on.

Guy gave his wife one final nervous grin.

"Listen to me," she responded. "You and I both know that this is the best idea we have ever had. This could put Calgary on the map. You have to go in there and make those men see that, too. It is now or never."

He kissed her quickly and left her in the hotel lobby on his way to attend the most important meeting of his life.

CHAPTER 13

◆◆◆◆◆

New Hybrids

$\mathcal{L}$ane, Cross, Burns, and McLean had all come to Alberta from elsewhere. George Lane was from the United States. Montreal-born Alfred Ernest Cross, a veterinary surgeon of the Ontario Agricultural College, had come to Calgary in 1884 to work for the British-American Horse Ranch Company. The following year he started his own ranch and in 1892 founded the Calgary Brewing and Malting Company. In 1899 he married the beautiful Helen (Nell) Macleod, daughter of Colonel James Macleod, of the North-West Mounted Police, who had established Fort Calgary in 1875. The Cross ranch, the a7 Ranche, near Nanton, is still owned by the Cross family and is still one of the largest ranches in the West. And if there ever was a man who could teach a cow to jump over the moon, it was the third character in this prairie epic: beef king Patrick Burns. An Irish immigrant, Burns owned a vast stock supply and processing industry and could have written a book on how to get rich on land and cattle. Finally, Archie McLean, who was appointed a minister in the Alberta provincial government in 1909, had come west from Ontario in 1886. McLean was not a true politician at heart—he had agreed to run for office only if he didn't have to campaign or make speeches. And he had another redeeming grace—he knew how to cowpunch before he entered politics and had worked his way to the top as a managing partner of the CY, the Cypress Cattle Company, near Taber, in southern Alberta.

That fateful day, George Lane summoned Patrick Burns, who also lived in the Alberta Hotel, and A. E. Cross to Lane's hotel room. The two men knew that whatever the meeting was about, it must have been important for him to ask them to the hotel in the middle of day. As they entered the room, Cross removed his cowboy hat and pitched it at the coat tree. Bull's eye. Patrick Burns, never without his trademark fedora, pushed up the brim of his hat and settled his considerable girth into one of the chairs surrounding the round table.

No cowboy could bring more skill and experience to this meeting than George Lane, and he knew it. Under his direction the 19,000-acre Bar U stocked over 3,000 head of cattle and 500 horses, including nearly 100 Percheron. With numbers like that, George Lane—a man who found animals easier to deal with than people—was aware of his power and figured it would be easy to get what he wanted from the two ranchers present.

"So what is going on?" asked A. E. Cross, checking the time on his pocket watch. "Why did you ask us here in the middle of the day?"

Lane stood and told them about his meeting with Weadick earlier that day. "Guy Weadick came to see me this morning with a pretty wild idea, but the more I listened, the more I began to think that he is crazy like a fox. He wants to add a rodeo to the Exhibition; he wants it to be the biggest outdoor show on earth. He wants Indians and women to be part of it. I haven't been able to think of anything else since I talked to him, and I have to tell you, the more I think about it, the more I believe it can work. But he needs investors, and that is where you two come in."

"I figured it would have something to do with my pocketbook," grumbled Cross.

"Give over, Alfred. You got more money than you know what to do with," said Burns.

Before Cross could reply, there was a knock at the door. Guy Weadick had arrived.

And unbeknownst to the men in the room, so had Florence. She couldn't help herself. She had secretly followed Guy up to the room and at that very moment was flattening herself against a hallway wall, waiting until Guy entered. Soon she would be kneeling in the hallway outside the room, her eyeball pressed to the keyhole, just as she used to do as a little girl when Colonel Cummins came calling. It was an undignified position, but with the stakes this high, her dignity was her last concern.

Guy entered the room, and after the obligatory introductions, Lane, Burns, and Cross took their places around the table. Guy stood before them, his ever-present cowboy hat firmly on his head.

Patrick Burns spoke first: "Well, Mr. Weadick, George Lane says that you have an interesting proposal for us. We would be most interested in hearing about it, so we would."

By this stage of his career, Guy Weadick was on a first-name basis with every performer and stock contractor from Canada to Mexico. He wore his celebrity easily and was smart about figuring out what people needed and wanted. And he had great intuition. He knew that if he was going to get his way, he had to come across as confident and strong. Begging and blustering would only make him seem weak. And he was determined not to crack even though those three faces, with their mouths in firm lines beneath bushy moustaches, were impassive and unreadable. It was now or never. He had learned long ago that when you really wanted to make your point, it was a better tactic to speak more softly than more strongly.

He summoned every ounce of nerve he had and began talking in his slow baritone. "See, what you got to understand is that back in 1893 the Chicago World's Fair was the turning point for us rodeo folks for two reasons. First off was the fact that it started out as a 400-year anniversary commemoration of Columbus's discovery of America. The official name of the celebration was the World's Columbian Exposition. Second, the American Historical Association had a meeting at the same time as the fair, and some university history professor by the name of Frederick Jackson Turner gave a lecture on how conquering the West had transformed the American character. I'm not much for names," said Weadick, "but I remember that one. Why? Because though we know the story is a lot mythical, he is keeping the Western ideal alive, and by doing that, he's giving rodeo promoters like me an audience."

Everyone knew about Turner's famous article, in which he argued that the Western frontier was "the meeting point between savagery and civilization." According to Turner, the frontier "begins with the Indian and the hunter; it goes on with the disintegration of savagery by the entrance of the trader . . . the pastoral stage in ranch life; the exploitation of the soil by the raising of unrotated crops of corn and wheat in sparsely settled farm communities; the intensive culture of the denser farm settlement; and finally the manufacturing organization with the city and the factory system." But it went beyond that: Turner saw the frontier as the front line in the creation of the American character, "that coarseness and strength combined with acuteness and acquisitiveness; that practical inventive turn of mind, quick to find expedients; that masterful grasp of material things . . . that restless, nervous energy; that dominant individualism." It was for him a place where men—and women—learned to rely on their smarts and their strengths. But was there an element of foreboding in his words? If American culture and democracy had been founded on frontier values, what would happen to these values as the frontier closed?

Guy knew that the three men sitting in front of him were aware of Turner. And he was sure that they agreed with his thesis and would apply it equally to the Canadian frontier. He was also sure that each of the three was profoundly attached to the West, to its rituals, its people, its occasional cruelty and frequent contradictions, its beauty and uniqueness, and that each wanted to preserve as much of it as he could.

He paused for effect and folded his arms across his chest. He figured that he had captured their attention. Now it was time to go in for the kill. He pushed his cowboy hat back on his head. "Second, people in Chicago said that if you hadn't seen Buffalo Bill's Real Wild West, you hadn't seen the fair. Those organizers said everything was all wrong with rodeo and refused to include it as part of the official fair. Anyone with a long-range view should see that an exhibition combined with a rodeo could complement each other perfectly. But Bill Cody wasn't even allowed on the premises in Chicago. So, out of spite, he single-handedly set up his extravaganza at the exhibition entrance on a lot between Sixty-second and Sixty-third Streets, and he had one helluva an audience. It was the most successful outdoor show in history, and Cody netted nearly one million dollars."

At that, the silence in the room hung heavy. Convinced he was coming out ahead, Weadick tilted his head down and looked at each of the three men in turn. One at a time, in almost perfect synchronization, Burns, Cross, and Lane moved forward onto their elbows.

"Hang on," asked Cross, always the one to speak up when money was being discussed. "How much money did you say?"

Weadick grabbed the back of a chair, sat down, and lowered his cowboy hat to eye level. When he spoke this time, his voice was deliberate and intense. "I said one million dollars. And where Cody was smart, was that he took advantage of a situation," he slowly continued. "And that is exactly what I am suggesting that you gentlemen do. Take advantage of the situation and me being ready, willing, and able to put on the finest rodeo on the continent, right here in Calgary, and to make our own rules."

"Rules like what?" asked George Lane, who already knew the answer to his question.

"Canadian rules with an emphasis on rodeo skills, not vaudeville," Weadick continued, "and the most money ever won is going to be here."

"What kind of money would you be thinking about, Mr. Weadick?" asked Patrick Burns, narrowing his eyes with the wariness of a self-made man. This was the part that Guy and Florence had mentally practised time and time again, and he could probably have said it in his sleep.

"If you can put up the financial sinews to underwrite the rodeo events for one hundred thousand dollars, I can give you a financial success like no other. We will have the most cowgirls and cowboys ever assembled in one place, and I will personally guarantee you will have over ten thousand spectators at the Exhibition."

The ranchers were dumbstruck, and Guy took advantage of the silence to press his point. "We need a parade. We need a parade like Earl Grey's in 1889, the Victoria Day parade of 1901, and that parade Calgary had in 1908, but this time I want to show where this country has come from and where it's headed. The parade would be in sequence to demonstrate the settlement of western Canada. We would have Hudson's Bay carts, stagecoaches, a squad of mounted policemen of 1874, and the present-day force. Hundreds of the finest cowboys and cowgirls, a reunion of old-time rangemen, ropers, bronco-twisters, and bulldoggers from across the West—from Old Mexico and New Mexico, Oregon, Utah, California, Wyoming, Montana, Colorado, Oklahoma, Arizona, Alberta, and British Columbia. I want to showcase the Treaty Seven nations and give them pride in their people and their past. We would have Indians, at least two thousand men with their women in traditional finery, papooses, travois. I believe that I can get the chiefs of the Stoney, Sarcee, and Blackfoot to agree to the presence of their people for the opening parade."

Lane figured that Archie McLean would find Weadick's idea preposterous. It was highly unlikely the government would ever agree to allow two thousand Indians to come off the reserve to ride horses through the streets of Calgary. Patrick Burns agreed. "Good God, man," he exclaimed, "we just now got them on their reserves!"

"Tell me something I don't know," retorted Weadick. "That won't stop me from going straight to the chiefs to tell them they could bring their tipis to the Exhibition grounds and set them up for the four-day run. I'd tell them they could bring their families in from the reserves to ride in the parade in full dress. They'll come, believe me," Weadick half bragged, "and if the government officials balk, they can deal with my wife."

"Your wife don't enter into this," George Lane harrumphed. Flores LaDue almost jumped through the keyhole when she heard this, but Guy did not miss a beat.

"With all due respect, sir," he was clearly trying to control his temper, "she more than does. Besides being able to ride and lasso better than anyone I know, man or woman, my wife grew up with the Sioux. She rode with the Sioux. She knows and appreciates them better than most, and she knows that a grave injustice has been done to those people. She's seen how a lot of those Wild West shows treat them, too, and she doesn't much care for it—the so-called savages killing women and children. The circus acts like one she saw just last year with an old Apache warrior, hero of a hundred battles with the whites, on the warpath killing his last buffalo with a bow and arrow from the seat of a speeding automobile. It is her and my sincere desire that in Calgary we shake that kind of performance from our boots."

"How so?" asked George Lane.

"Show their native dances and ceremonies and make sure they are treated with the respect that is their due," Weadick said quietly. "But that's not all. I want Western art. I intend to invite a certain Mr. Charlie Russell and a certain Mr. Ed Borein up here to sell some of their paintings. And as far as rodeo events are concerned, we want the whole ball of wax or nothing at all. We want bucking horse riding events for cowgirls at the Calgary Stampede. My wife says there is no good reason why women like her and Lucille Mulhall can't compete here in trick and fancy roping like they have at Los Angeles, Pendleton, Cheyenne, and Winnipeg." He took a breath. "And we want cowgirls in the relay races, too."

Oklahoma cowgirl Lucille Mulhall was one of the best-known Western performers of her era and the woman Will Rogers had dubbed "the world's first cowgirl." Lucille began her career performing in her father's Wild West show and later became one of the most accomplished riding and roping champions, competing against and sometimes beating male competitors in steer roping events. Lucille helped make women an integral part of rodeo.

Weadick's declaration was met with guffaws.

"Cowgirls! The wild horses have yet to be born that could drag us to agree with that idea!" said Burns, "Those relay riders have to change horses at record speed at the end of the first and second laps. No way can we change rules for women. To play fair with the cowboys, they would have to unsaddle each horse and saddle the next one before each of the three laps. No woman I know can race relays."

At that Cross cleared his throat. "Incorrect," he said, "my wife can." Indeed, Nell Cross could ride as well as any man, and if she'd been in the room with this quartet, she would have set them straight. There was a moment of somewhat embarrassed muttering, then Burns asked Weadick what else he was proposing for the Stampede.

"Roman riding," he said with a smile. "Rodeo women race

standing astride two horses at full gallop the whole doggone time."

The usual jovial Burns leaned forward on his elbows and sighed. "We'll be cartin' women off to the morgue by the dozen, so we will."

"I don't think so, Mr. Burns." Guy paused briefly. "I tell you what. Come watch my wife and her rodeo friends audition so you can see for yourself. One thing for sure, we are not going to get bogged down in a quagmire of bone-dry rodeo. There'll be entertainment for everyone. We all want the same thing, don't we? A celebration and re-creation of the authentic atmosphere of the frontier that will also make a little money." He was encouraged to see the three men nod in agreement. He then threw in the ace he'd been saving for last.

"One more thing, gentlemen. I think you will be pleased to learn that I've been talking to representatives of the Canadian Pacific Railway. I may be putting the cart before the horse here"—Weadick grinned—"but I've told them that if I can cut a deal with you gentlemen, they would have a huge tourist attraction here. If the Stampede deal goes through, the CPR has promised to offer half-price round-trip fares to Calgary, and that could bring thousands of tourists to this city. We'll fill up the stands, and even have people clear down on each side."

George Lane knew he had to persuade Burns and Cross to take this deal, but to do so, he had to talk to them privately.

"Wait for us in the foyer, will you, Guy? We won't be long."

On the other side of the door, Florence Weadick stood up so fast she almost fainted. She'd been crouching so long her knees were shaking and her back was aching. As she balanced and straightened her skirts, she noticed a hotel housekeeper walking toward her with a pile of towels. It was showtime again.

"Excuse me, ma'am, I seem to have got myself all turned around," Florence said. "I'm looking for the foyer." The woman pointed in the obvious direction. How odd, she thought, the hotel wasn't so big that someone could get lost in it.

Back inside, before he took leave of the men who held his future in their hands, Guy Weadick planted both his hands on the table, leaned forward, and looked each one square in the eye.

"Remember, gentlemen, close only counts in horseshoes."

CHAPTER 14

◆◆◆◆◆

George Lane Circles the Wagons

George Lane had a roaring headache. He could outride, out-rope, and outshoot most men, but he couldn't outtalk many of them. He had always been more interested in action than words, and in steers than people; he was sure that he hadn't heard so much yapping in years. At the same time, although Guy Weadick talked a lot, he had a lot of good things to say, and Lane found himself on Weadick's side. Now all he had to do was convince the others.

"Every darn one of us knows that Weadick is right when he says that the plough, barbed-wire fencing, and the railway have ruined the open-range life of the cowboy. All due respect to you, Pat," he said, nodding at Patrick Burns, "once the railway was completed and new ways of refrigeration and packing allowed beef to be shipped efficiently across North America, the era of long cattle drives, riding herds, breaking wild horses, and traditional work roundups for cowboys pretty much came to an end. Oh, there are some of those big corporate ranches that still take on cowboys, but all's many city folks know about the West is what they read in books and see in moving pictures, whatever the blazes they are."

Burns and Cross looked thoughtful.

"In my view, the man that just walked out of this room is the one to put this thing together," Lane continued, gesturing toward to the closed door. "And as far as the women are concerned," he continued, "if you think that you can ask Guy Weadick not to include women at the first Calgary Stampede, then you haven't met his wife."

Patrick Burns seemed unimpressed: "One of my hired hands told me that he watched Guy Weadick and Florence LaDue entertain in the infield here at the 1908 Exhibition and he figured he looked like some kinda fancy-pants, half scared of his wife."

A. E. Cross straightened his tie and avoided the eyes of the others: "Let's admit it," he said, certain that his wife would discourage ladies from attending a Stampede showcasing cowgirls riding broncos, "we're all half scared of our wives."

"Well, we can stumble around or draw the women in," replied Lane, whose Alberta-born wife, Elizabeth, had grown up in High River and was highly knowledgeable about cowgirl subculture. "I have faith in Guy Weadick's skills of persuasion in getting reporters from the *Calgary Herald* to cover the ladies' events with photos, interviews, and fair stories."

"If we each put in twenty-five thousand dollars, would Archie McLean contribute the same amount?" Cross asked.

"Absolutely guaranteed," assured Patrick Burns, who had established a lasting friendship with McLean back in the 1880s, in Winnipeg, where both had established successful businesses in conjunction with the CPR.

"Good," said George Lane, "I'll send him an invoice. So, gentlemen, what'll it be? Are you in or out?"

"In" said Cross.

"Me, too," said Burns.

"That's it. Only thing missing is the handshake," said Lane. "Let's find Weadick and give him the news. There is one more thing, though. Money aside—if this thing does go ahead, there may be resistance. Folks here know that Weadick is from New York, and some may not accept an American promoter as the organizer of the first Stampede. So we need to know what to say to such people, and I think it is this—by the 1880s, at the Bar U and other outfits like it, almost all of the foremen working on Canadian corporate ranches were experienced American cowboys like me. From start to finish, most Calgarians are hybrids. Best comparison I can think of is the Texas longhorn. In the late 1880s they were the easiest keeper but sorriest excuse for a beef animal known to man. Later they were graded-up and bred to high-grade bulls for better beef quality. Canadians did the same when we crossbred longhorns to Hereford or Angus shorthorns from Britain, and in the process we got ourselves the best beef. And a Calgarian ain't no different. Don't matter if he's wearin' chaps or jodhpurs, he's got the best of American and British standards. So it's my bet that if we hire Weadick, he won't be the first or the last American to become a Calgarian. Hell, I'm one myself."

The other men nodded.

"So, let's go tell Weadick our decision."

They grabbed their hats and headed toward the foyer in a side-by-side formation, with George Lane in the middle.

Guy and Florence jumped to their feet as the three men approached; they didn't know what to think—the men looked so grim, especially Cross, whose expression was almost dark. But the Weadicks knew better than to second-guess. Appearances are terribly deceiving sometimes, so they waited, and as the three men approached, George Lane stuck his hand out and said, "Mr. Weadick, you got yourself a Stampede."

Guy Weadick didn't know whose hand to shake first, so he tried to shake them all while Florence stood beside him and beamed.

Perhaps from a distance, this group of four prosperous-looking men and one elegant cowgirl gathered together in the foyer of the Alberta Hotel might have looked like ordinary people, but they weren't. In the course of one day, they had all sealed a place for themselves in Alberta's history. Florence and Guy Weadick's names would forever be associated with what was and has always since been the greatest outdoor show on earth, as have the names Burns, Cross, Lane, and McLean, whom Calgarians forever after would call the Big Four.

As they parted company with plans to meet with the Exhibition board of directors the following day to arrange for the use of the grounds at Victoria Park, they told Guy Weadick they would take him to the bank afterward. They also told him this: "Make the Calgary Stampede the best event of its kind in the world. We don't want to lose money if we can help it, but we'd rather lose money and have it right than make money and have it wrong."

CHAPTER 15

◆◆◆◆◆

The First Calgary Exhibition and Stampede 1912: A Star Is Born

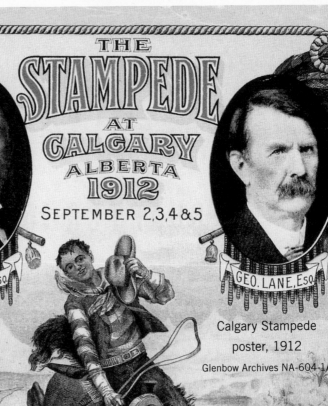

Calgary Stampede
poster, 1912

Glenbow Archives NA-604-1A

The second half of Florence and Guy Weadick's life started that evening when they moved into the Alberta Hotel. The following day Cross, Burns, and Lane took Guy Weadick to Victoria Park to meet the Exhibition's board of directors and, in an awesome display of arm twisting, arranged for the use of the Exhibition grounds. Then they went to the bank. With a contribution of $25,000 from each man—with McLean contributing the same amount in absentia—a $100,000 account was opened in the name of Frontier Days Celebration Committee. They gave Guy Weadick a chequebook and appointed him general manager with duties to "manage, produce, and publicize the event." Though he had rejected Guy's proposal, Ernie Richardson was appointed as the financial treasurer, an arrangement that began a twenty-year working relationship between him and Weadick, who bore the older man no grudge for his earlier rejection of Guy's proposition. H. R. McMullen, as the official director general, began to organize the parade, and Reverend John McDougall was deputized for a fee of $390 and told to gather all the First Nations peoples from southern Alberta.

Now all Guy had to do was get the acts together.

Weadick was well aware of the power of celebrity. He fired

off invitations across the continent promising all-time highs in championship money that were enthusiastically accepted by the rodeo illuminati, artists Ed Borein and Charlie Russell, hundreds of First Nations people, some rather renowned cowgirls, such as award-winning broncobuster and world-champion relay racer Fannie Sperry, who was handed a letter in the post office north of her family ranch in Helena, Montana. Twenty-five-year old Sperry was a beautiful, tall, blue-eyed brunette who had competed for numerous rodeo championships alongside Florence LaDue. Her remarkable rodeo riding skills had won her the respect of champion cowboys and cowgirls alike, and she smiled to herself as she scanned the letter while imagining her friend Florence commanding her husband, in the nicest of possible ways, to "take a letter."

> *Dear Miss Sperry:*
>
> *I'm impressed with your bronc riding. If you can come to the Stampede I'm putting on in Calgary September 2–5, 1912, I'm sure you can win some big money. You'll be riding for the world's championship.*
>
> *Guy Weadick*

Guy's trump card, though, was Prince Arthur, the Duke of Connaught and Strathearn, the Governor General of Canada. Along with his wife, the Duchess of Connaught, and their popular daughter, Princess Patricia, the royal party planned to be in Calgary around the time of the Stampede, and Guy Weadick extended the dates by two days to accommodate them. The endorsement of the British royals and plans to construct special royal boxes at the Exhibition grounds got Weadick so excited that he overplayed his hand with an understaffed committee trying to meet a deadline when he told them that he also wanted to invite King George V. This request was met with a hailstorm of his own promotional brochures, entry forms, telegrams, and full-page newspapers with the headline "The Stampede, a Reunion of Old Timers in the Great West" being flung at his head and fluttering to the floor in the hallway as the office door was slammed in his face. Florence, who had been waiting for him at office reception, sagged against the wall, unable to stop laughing as she glanced back and forth between her husband and the mountain of paper surrounding him.

"Guy Weadick," she said, "your problem is that you are beginning to believe your own bullshit."

By late May 1912, Guy Weadick had everything under control. He had arranged for old whisky trader Fred Kanouse to work with a committee to set up replicas of Fort Whoop-Up, a Hudson Bay post, and other side events. The program was also finalized: Stampede grandstand performances would start every day at one o'clock in the afternoon and in the evening at eight thirty, and all world championships would take place at the open-air grandstand or in the covered arena at the grounds. Tickets would go on sale in August. There would be a total of 40,000 free rush seats in the temporary bleachers encircling the entire racetrack; general admission cost one dollar. Other prices were fifty cents for reserved grandstand seats and sixty dollars for boxes containing six seats. As for publicity, Guy and Florence handled that personally by setting out on a promotional tour to southern Alberta and the United States. If anyone could entice rodeo stock owners, competitors, performers, and skilled behind-the-scenes rodeo workers to Calgary, it was Guy

Stampede parade, 1912

Glenbow Archives NA-4035-96

Weadick himself. After all, hadn't his wife told him on more than one occasion that his initials G. W. stood for Good with Words? En route they stopped at reserves to invite the Indians. The *Calgary Daily Herald* and its advertisers were onside from the beginning and bombarded readers with full-page spreads:

THE STAMPEDE—CALGARY, ALBERTA, CANADA—SEPTEMBER 2-3-4-5-6 & 7, 1912

ONE WHOLE WILD DELIRIOUS WEEK—The city turned over to cowboys, cowgirls, riders, ropers, Mexican vaqueros, guides, scouts, Royal North-West Mounted Policemen, miners, packers, and frontiersmen of all kinds, Indian Chiefs and their tribes. Grandest Galaxy of western types ever gathered anywhere. $20,000 in cash prizes. Information headquarters—706A Centre Street, Guy Weadick, Manager.

The flood of advertising warned Calgarians who wished to ride in the daily parade that they must be attired in cowboy or cowgirl costumes and have stock, Western saddles, chaps, fancy coloured mufflers, shirts, and Stetson hats ready in plenty of time. And thanks to Flores LaDue, the old saw "It's a man's world" was about to change: on August 24, 1912, the *Daily Herald* published its first-ever illustration of a cowgirl playfully advertising the Stampede.

Work continued at a feverish pace from spring till September. Finally, after six months of preparation, the Calgary Stampede graduated from a promise into a reality. And it began with a parade. Never had such a pageant of amazing sights, sounds, and smells passed through the streets of Calgary. Florence and Guy Weadick gloried in parading past the Big Four—George

Lane, Patrick Burns, A. E. Cross, and Archie McLean—who stood proudly on the viewing stand. Florence and Guy led a cavalcade of 2,000 Indians, the greatest cowboys and cowgirls of the world, the Royal North-West Mounted Police, who were joined in the pomp and ceremony by every attraction and person who had witnessed life on the plains. Eighty thousand people lined the parade route, and it was said that the only ones who missed the parade were either in hospital or jail.

The crowds followed the parade down to the Exhibition grounds, and the grand show began. The 1912 *Calgary Daily Herald* described it this way:

Director General Harry McMullen is a very pleased man. The evening performance commenced with a general parade of the performers headed by Guy Weadick, H. G. McMullen. The Pendleton, Oregon, Mounted Band received the greatest ovation as they led the party into the arena, and the individuals came in for considerable notice as they proceeded round the ring. There were about 50 of the finest horsewomen and men in the world, each one an expert in several branches of range work. Miss Arline Palmer gave a splendid exhibition of Cossack riding, and the manner in which she careered round the ring on almost every place on the horse but the saddle evoked great applause. Miss Dolly Mullin gave a few examples of what a girl can do on a horse when she changed her seat from time to time while at the gallop and then rode round the ring with her head almost sweeping the ground. Otto Kline performed some hair-raising stunts in the saddle from galloping with head to the ground to dismounting and mounting on the move, and landing on the off-side of his mount. Kline is surely the best trick rider ever seen in Calgary if not the whole American continent. His exhibition of mail carrying and express work was splendid and brought rounds of applause from veterans of the range. Numbers of artists gave rope twirling, noosing and roping exhibitions—perhaps in this line the most noted being Tex McLeod, who roped five horses and riders at one throw, and the men from Mexico, the Mexican vaqueros, brought off some wonderful work, the best being when one of them, on foot, lassoed a pony and dropped it with the rope only attached to his leg. Nine Indian Chiefs rode round the ring and gave exhibitions of Indian riding, which augmented by their wonderful costumes, delighted all present. Taken all through, the show is remarkable.

The relay races were crowd favourites—in these races cowboys charged around the track at breakneck speed, changing their mounts at the end of each half-mile lap. To do this, they had to rein their horse to a sudden and abrupt halt, leap off, jerk off the saddle and blanket, put them on their other horse, and get away again as fast as they could. Switching saddles from one horse to the other shows the ordinary everyday rider just how quickly it is possible to saddle a horse.

The Indian encampment, full of tipis erected by the Piikani, Kainai, Siksika, Tsuu T'ina, and Stoney-Nakoda aroused enormous interest. One *Calgary Daily Herald* editorial had this to say:

The Indian department of the Dominion Government has granted permission to the Indian to take part in the Stampede celebrations next month. . . . It should not be forgotten that he is the representative of a great race—a race remarkable for many sovereign qualities of a remote and picturesque past. He should be treated with dignity and respect and the department should have no reason to regret the permission it has granted to help make Calgary's festival a remarkable success.

Tom Three Persons was listening. The only Canadian left in the bronc riding finals, he was a twenty-five-year-old Blood Indian from Cardston who was pretty skilled at protecting himself. He had quick eyes, good moves, fast hands—characteristics that Glen Campbell, the inspector for the Indian agencies for the Dominion government, had seen Tom Three Persons display in rodeo competitions on the circuit and that he wanted to see again at the first Calgary Stampede. Unfortunately, Tom Three

Tipis at Indian Village, Stampede grounds, 1912

Persons was nowhere to found. He was cooling his heels behind the stone walls of the Fort Macleod jail, where he was a guest of His Majesty after overindulging in pre-Stampede spirit. In short order, Campbell, whom Stampede management thanked for the presence of thousands of Indians, arranged to have him sprung from jail and rushed up to Calgary. Tom Three Persons knew that this was his once-in-a-lifetime opportunity, and he was not about to disappoint. But he hadn't met Cyclone yet. For seven years, this supposedly unrideable black equine demon, nick-named the Black Terror, had been tossing anyone who had tried to ride him, and by the time he'd been shipped from Oklahoma to Calgary, he'd tossed 127 riders overboard.

Though it is hard to believe looking at the Stampede grounds today, back in 1912 there were no chutes or pens to saddle the bucking stock. Instead wild horses were roped and snubbed to the saddle horn of the roper's horse in the middle of the arena. And there was no eight-second rule. As long as the cowboy—or girl—could sit in the saddle, they would continue riding until the horse quit bucking. One can imagine that there were a lot of sore cowpunchers back in those days.

Tom Three Persons had noticed that once the animals were released, most steer roping, bulldogging, and bronc riding stock took off for the far side of the infield. He was to ride last, and he didn't plan to have spectators confuse his performance with a chess game. Cyclone proved impossible to saddle, because he would rear and throw himself backward only to pitch forward and land ferociously on all fours.

Getting a cowboy or cowgirl on a bucking horse took forever, and the day that Tom Three Persons drew Cyclone was no ex-ception. For half an hour, ropers chased the bucker from one end of the field to another, a tedious exercise that was beginning to draw some boos from the Stampede spectators. Finally, Tom saw that officials had cornered Cyclone long enough to hold him down on the ground and saddle him right in front of the grandstand crowd. They signalled Tom to come forward, position himself over the horse, and get his feet in the stirrups. He did so with great apprehension. Before Tom knew it, Cyclone got up. He later described his ride to Albertan newspaperman Fred Kennedy, who wrote in *The Albertan*:

> Cyclone wasn't too tough when he was buckin' straight ahead. But when he sucked back and started to raise in front, he

440 · CHIEFS OF THE STONEYS, SARCEES AND BLACKFEET WITH GUY WEADICK, STAMPEDE CHIEF. - © W.J.OLIVER.

Guy Weadick, shown here with the chiefs of the Stoneys, Sarcees, and Blackfeet, at the first Calgary Stampede, 1912

Glenbow Archives NB-16-401

could balance on one hind leg better 'n any bronc I had ever seen. Well he starts to raise with me after the fifth jump, and scared the hell right out of me. I thought he was coming over backwards. Without realizing what I was really doin', I started to beller at him. He was so surprised that he flattened out. I knew I had 'im then so I just kept on spurring until I rode him to a standstill. The thing that I can remember best about that ride was that the band kept playing the same tune over and over and people kept singing. I asked Guy Weadick what they were singing. He said, 'There will be a hot time in the old town tonight.' And there sure as hell was.

History would be good to Tom Three Persons—he became a trailblazer and a role model for many talented professional Native cowboys. And through his ranching activities, he became one of the wealthiest Native people in the country.

The Ladies Take the Stage

History would also be good to the cowgirls of the first Calgary Stampede. Before 1912, press coverage of women's events had been minimal and biased. Now they would finally take their rightful place alongside the men. In the women's bronc riding championship, the main competition was between Fanny Sperry and an Alberta cowgirl named Goldie St. Clair, whose first mount was a sorrel named Red Wing; a cowboy had accidentally been killed by Red Wing just days before the Stampede began, so emotions were running high. The two women were tied until the third day of competition—this time Sperry

Ladies at the Stampede, 1912

Glenbow Archives NA-335-14

drew Red Wing, and gained the edge on St. Clair, who wore stirrups for her ride, while Sperry did not. By riding slick saddle like a man, the judges considered Sperry to be a much better rider, because she did not deign to hobble the stirrups by tying them together beneath the horse like most women did. She won the day and became the Lady Bucking Horse Champion of the World, for which she was awarded $1,000.

Next came the relay races; Flores LaDue was entered in

this event but lost in the free-for-all of the two-mile relay race, where her small stature was a disadvantage. The multitalented Bertha Blancett, who competed in all four official women's events, won the relay race. But Flores LaDue wasn't done yet. There was still the trick roping competition. All the contestants were to rope each day and to be prepared to exhibit their skills at the beck and call of the arena director at any time during the performance. Contestants were judged on the variety of their tricks, ease, gracefulness, and general skill. Flores wasn't worried about her skill. She could rope a fly off the wall and was the first woman to flawlessly execute the trick known as the Texas Skip, which involved spinning the loop vertically and jumping through it from side to side. She could keep sixty-five feet of rope suspended in midair at one time. Hadn't a *New York Times* reporter said she was a performer seemingly possessed with magic? What she could not do on a horse or with a rope was not worth mentioning.

By one o'clock in the afternoon on the day of the roping competition, the Duke of Connaught and the royal party had arrived at the grandstand in the drizzling rain; within the hour it was decided to move the entire rodeo over to the indoor horse show building even though that facility had fewer than half the number of seats of the grandstand and bleachers. The resulting mini-stampede included a not-so-hilarious scene of the royal party having to elbow their way into the facility along with the muddy masses. Over half the spectators did not get in and did not get their money back. The following day the *Calgary Daily Herald* published a scathing editorial stating that the afternoon and evening performances of the Calgary Stampede had been nothing but "a perfect bungle from beginning to end." But in the pelting rain, what was the alternative? Ropes don't fly quite so high in a downpour.

So, on September 5, 1912, the fancy roping and trick riding competitions got under way at eight thirty in the evening; it was obvious to all that the main competition was going to be between Flores LaDue and Lucille Mulhall.

Earlier Mulhall had performed in the men's steer roping event—there were no other women to compete with her in that category—and she hadn't been shy to brag about being the only woman at the Stampede who could rope, throw, and tie a steer. In fact, she'd been asked to give the crowd a demonstration of her skills. Everyone, including Florence, was in awe of her ability to seemingly drop her rope through space onto the horns of a running wild steer, coolly upend the animal, and throw it to the ground. Her horse seemed by instinct to know what was taking place and what to do at the right moment. Once Mulhall dismounted and ran forward to the steer, her horse tightened the stretch of rope, intervening and tugging away, holding and dragging the steer until Lucille had him securely tied. All of this in fifty-two seconds.

After Mulhall's magnificent demonstration in the infield that day, Florence couldn't believe her ears when she heard a newspaper reporter ask Guy if steer roping was really something that women would do.

"Anyone who goes to throw a steer is taking his life in his hands. He runs every danger of being gored or having the steer turn on him and get him in a position where he is sure of fatal injury. There are many times in ranch life when a cowpuncher finds it necessary to handle a steer in this way. The Stampede aims to give a complete picture of ranch life and practice— whether it's done by a cowboy or a cowgirl."

Enough said.

Now here was Flores competing against this amazing woman whom the *Calgary Daily Herald* had dubbed the "defending world champion." As Flores stood by her husband in the infield that afternoon, she knew that her roping competition with Mulhall was going to be close. But if anyone should take the coveted first prize of a $1,000 and a brand-new saddle in trick roping, Florence LaDue Weadick knew it was just this side of possible that it would be her.

The building was filled to capacity. Spectators wanted their money's worth, and she was going to give it to them. Lucille Mulhall performed first. As expected, her act was excellent. Then, as Flores heard her name being called over the megaphone, she rode her liver chestnut gelding into the infield, her back straight and her face bearing a determined smile. She knew she had to be better than excellent.

A thunderous cheer arose, and she responded by doffing her Stetson in appreciation. It was showtime. And what a show she put on. First, with two seemingly slight movements of her tiny wrists, she tied a double hitch in her slackened rope. Next, to show her famous agility, she instantly flipped her rope to do the double-looped Pretzel followed by her trademark Overhand.

She knew that her next routine was outrageous, but she was determined to show it—she hadn't spent months practising it for nothing. She planned to catch some horses—not on horseback or on foot, but by lying flat on her back in the infield.

To do this, she dismounted in one smooth motion. Her horse cantered off to stand by the rail while Florence remained in the centre of the infield, like a solitary figure in a landscape painting. Then to the astonishment of all those watching, this young woman wearing buckskin and silk sank down in the dirt and lay on her back. Her tiny feet wore black appliqué boots, and at the other end of her body a mass of thick dark hair spread out on her Stetson. In her right hand she held a rope with a six-foot loop; in her left she held the long control end of the rope. She lay motionless and soon a hush came over the spectators as a rangy young cowboy and his big bay rode through a chute onto the infield and began to gallop toward her at a frightening speed. Flores could hear the mare's hoofbeats and used the sound to calculate its distance from her. She then stretched her back upward as if a chinook wind had lifted her spine into an arch. Her head bent back so that the on-coming horse and rider were now in her line of vision.

When the mare was ten feet away from Flores's head, the rider yanked the reins to the right so as to have the bay circle around the motionless speck of a woman. Above her, Flores La-Due saw nothing but the curved beams of the arena roof as she waited until the last possible second. Her timing would have to be perfect. Suddenly, quiet as a striking rattler, she flicked the wide loop across her body and landed it around one hind foot of the running horse. Immediately, the rope released so as not to trip the animal, and the horse veered away from her, shower-ing her with dust. It was a stunning display of skill and drew a tumultuous ovation.

She was not finished, though. She stood up, brushed herself off, and almost before the crowd realized it, she had lassoed five thundering horses abreast. But she was not content with that; after one of the riders dismounted, smiled in resignation, waved his hat to the audience, and began to saunter over toward Flores, she lassoed him, too, and tied him up, hand and foot, with three quick motions of her wrist.

With her clever handwork and rope handling skill, with her poise and determination, Flores LaDue had outroped all her competitors; she had reached the pinnacle of her career. With a feminine calm she gathered her ropes hand over hand and walked over to stand before the horses and riders. She smiled as she turned to face the crowd and slowly raised her arms in victory. Overhead the twisted strands of her lariat formed tumbling garlands trailing downward through her gloved fingers.

The deluge of applause started with one appreciative person in the audience standing and clapping. Soon, others joined in until everyone in bench seating was on their feet acknowledging that Flores LaDue had won the championship. Guy Weadick proudly beckoned his wife to the stage. He picked up the leather belt with its championship engraved gold buckle and wrapped it around her tiny waist, which was so small, the belt went around twice. He then angled his head toward the megaphone and said, "And that's not all." He walked over to the saddle stand to a magnificent saddle engraved with a sterling silver plaque on the back of the cantle. He picked it up, walked over to his wife, and presented her with the saddle.

"Ladies and gentlemen, it sure is a pleasure for me to present this award. As most of you know, I happen to know the winner quite well. She's been my wife for six years. And I don't mind telling you that the first time I saw her I fell in love with her. Even though she happened to be upside down at the time. I guess you could say I was head over heels from the minute I saw her."

The crowd was loving every minute of Guy's speech. Flores was, too.

"I have never seen a woman do with a rope what this here

Florence LaDue Weadick, Champion Lady Fancy Roper of
the World, 1912, shown here with her inordinate amount of
rope and its perfectly placed honda eyelet at the end

Glenbow Archives NA-335-21

little woman can do, with the possible exception of Miss Lucille
Mulhall." Lucille, who was watching from the sidelines, smiled
and nodded her head at Guy. "And I don't mind admitting, that
when I watched my wife lasso and tie up that cowboy, I said to
myself, 'Son, I know the feeling.' "

At this, the crowd roared, and Florence gave Guy a mock

kick on the shin. She knew his sense of showmanship required this moment; besides, she was enjoying herself.

"So, before I get myself into any more hot water, ladies and gentlemen, I present to you World Champion Lady Fancy Roper, Flores LaDue."

Then, almost like conspirators, the Weadicks smiled at each other. Guy grabbed his wife by the waist and bent her over backward. "I've always been a sucker for a lady with a lariat," he whispered into her thick dark hair.

Guy stopped talking and looked at thirteen-year-old Lenore. She had stopped crying but her eyes were red and her face a little swollen. She would be okay, though. She would have to be. Life and death are part of the grand scheme, and as a child growing up on a ranch, Lenore knew that very well. He kissed her on top of her head, said goodbye to Josephine, and left the Bews ranch with a heavy heart. Two months later, Florence's fervent wish for him came true—he was asked to ride in the 1952 Calgary Stampede parade. Still charming and likeable, he gave out awards as well and was gratified to see that prizes had doubled since his day and also that the chuck-wagon races, his idea, had become the most popular event next to the saddle bronc riding.

The next year, in 1953, Guy Weadick passed suddenly. At the funeral, Guy's boots were put backward in the stirrups of his horse, Snip, who walked riderless. Guy was buried next to his beloved Florence, side by side for eternity in that small cemetery under the gaze of the Rocky Mountains, on the southern Alberta plain that they both loved so much.

CHAPTER 16

◆◆◆◆◆

The Big Four
Would Approve

Though one hundred years have passed, Guy Weadick, Patrick Burns, A. E. Cross, Archie McLean, and George Lane would undoubtedly still recognize many components of their Stampede were they to visit it today. The magic they created in 1912 has passed largely untouched through the decades.

A century later, people around the world continue their love affair with animals in a relationship and partnership that extends from companionship and recreation, to work and sport—and the Stampede remains a celebration of that ongoing relationship. Throughout the ten-day festival, about 7,500 animals are involved in dozens of exhibitions, as well as in educational and competitive events. For many city folks, the Stampede is their only chance to see animals in action. For the Stampede and those showcasing their animals, it's a chance to proudly display their great passion for animal welfare.

The grandstand, the rodeo arena, and the agriculture barns are still located on the banks of the meandering Elbow River. The Big Four would appreciate that agriculture is still an important focus of the organization, and there are dozens of committees and hundreds of volunteers representing many sectors of that industry. With respect to the Park itself, the original acreage forms its core, and over the years land has been added to accommodate growth. The community of Victoria Park has been absorbed within the Park's boundaries and is the site of major development projects that will take the organization into the next century as a cornerstone of Calgary's vibrant inner-city life.

Guy Weadick would be tickled pink to see Weadickville, an oasis of authentic Western buildings named in his honour, located on the west side of the Park. And all of them, Guy and the Big Four alike, would marvel at the numbers—1.2 million people pass through the gates during the annual Stampede. The Indian Village mirrors the original encampment in 1912, and each year tens of thousands of visitors experience the traditional culture of the Treaty 7 First Nations.

Some things have changed, of course. In 1912, most cowboys who competed in the rodeo earned their living working on ranches and farms. Today, the cowboys who are invited to compete are professionals who have risen to the highest level of their sport. The purses they compete for echo Guy's generous prizes at the original Stampede, when there was $20,000 cash on offer. Now the Stampede provides the richest regular-season rodeo in the world, and $100,000-plus day money is won by the top competitors in each event.

Honouring Guy Weadick's desire to connect the community to its cultural roots through a spirit of celebration, over the next few years an ambitious development plan will transform Stampede Park. A new Main Street featuring galleries, shopping, and restaurants will provide a destination area for Calgarians and tourists alike. River Park will be created in the northeast quadrant of the Park to provide a rare and unique natural inner-city oasis for the benefit of all. The authentic and historic Indian Village will be relocated within River Park. A new state-of-the-art agriculture arena and exhibit hall has been designed and will welcome agricultural events and exhibitors year round.

One hundred years on, Guy Weadick and the Big Four would approve.

EPILOGUE

◆◆◆◆◆

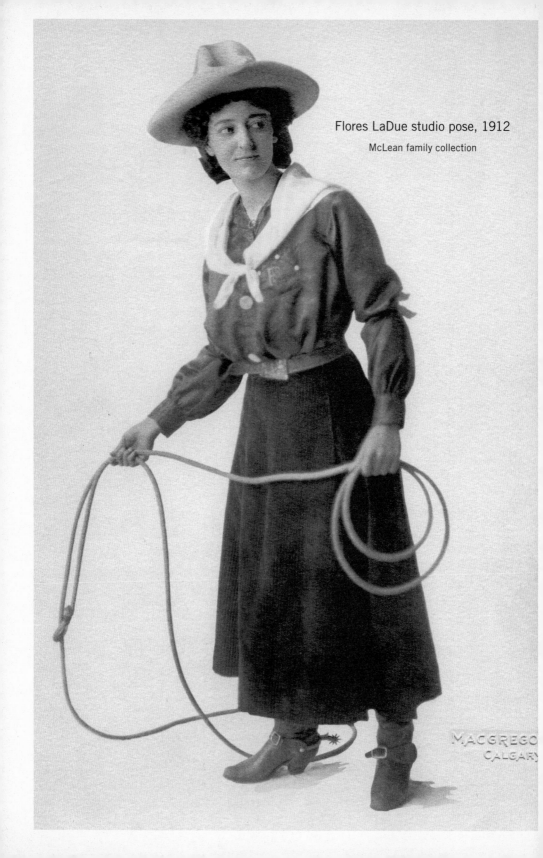

Flores LaDue studio pose, 1912

McLean family collection

It's September 2001, fifty years after the death of Florence LaDue Weadick, and the flat Alberta prairie and hollowed-out gullies of the McLean ranch reach out in all directions like a friendly palm. A dark-haired woman is riding Super Cowgirl, a sorrel mare with a strip of white down her face and two white socks, on a Longview ranch, when the cell phone in her vest pocket rings, and the horse lays back her ears at the intrusive sound. Lenore Bews McLean swears to herself at the interruption and keeps riding straight ahead, her eyes searching the vast horizon as she gathers cattle. After a period of silence, the phone rings again, and again she ignores it. Lenore brings her horse to a halt at the crest of a hill. As she rocks in the saddle the reflection of the Alberta sun bounces off the engraved silver plaque on its back.

FLORES LADUE
WORLD'S CHAMPION LADY FANCY ROPER

The saddle was made by Claude Mills—back in the day he was the best in the business—and when Lenore rode in it, she felt that it connected her over time and space to the woman who had been her advisor, guide, inspiration, model, and, in a way, muse. The connection between them was almost uncanny and they had so much in common. Although Lenore did not grow up on a Sioux reservation like Mrs. Weadick did, she, too, felt a strong connection with and empathy for aboriginal people, especially the Stoney Indians from the nearby Morley Reserve. Her father had told her that if it had not been for the Indians working on the ranches in the summer, many ranchers in Longview and the surrounding district would have been long gone. And in the spring they would come. Over the foothills in a line of pageantry and bright colours, the women walking or riding alongside horse-drawn Democrat wagons brimming with children, just as they had decades before when they had gone to the Weadicks' ranch. And at the head of the procession the men still proudly rode their horses at a slow jog. Lenore was always so happy to see the Indian children—she saw no difference between herself and the children from Morley. During the summer she would be invited to their camp where she learned their ways, such as eating pemmican, a pounded dried meat mixed with berries. In late summer, when the leaves began to turn golden and fall, Lenore would grow sad knowing that her playmates would soon head back to the reserve. When Lenore's father, Joe Bews, passed away in 1982, many people from Morley filled the church pews at the funeral. After Lenore thanked them for attending, Vera Daniels, a survivor of the sad chapter in Canadian history when Indian children were separated from their families and placed in residential schools, told her: "We are family, and family is there when you need them."

In some intangible way, Florence LaDue Weadick was always with Lenore, wherever she went—in the corrals and the range of the McLean ranch, in the splendid country west of Longview, and in the nursery and kitchen of the ranch house.

Mrs. Weadick had once told her that she had better learn as much as possible about cooking and housework. Although Florence could do things with a lariat that almost no one else on earth could, she was a wife, too, and she had learned to cook and clean house as a young girl. She had always taken seriously her wifely duties to look after her husband, and she thought that Lenore should, too.

"I don't care," Lenore had declared. "When I grow up I'm going to have a maid," to which Mrs. Weadick retorted, "You'd better know all you can so you can keep a check on the maid."

There had been no maid, even when the McLeans ran a guest ranch for a few years.

Sometimes when Lenore is out here riding alone and the air is still and the light is right, she feels the presence of Mrs. Weadick riding beside her on Somber, her pretty liver chestnut-coloured gelding. In fact, one summer day just a few weeks before, Lenore had ridden out with a picnic lunch for the hired hands, who were getting the hay off. It was so hot that she lay down under the relentless sun, slid her cowboy hat over her face, and fell asleep, and Mrs. Weadick came to her in her dream, looking as spectacular as she always had in real life, with her suede jacket, split skirt, and long, leather, beaded and fringed riding gloves. And, of course, her wonderful little black boots.

For some reason, Lenore held her hands in front of herself and turned them over several times; they were not the delicate hands of the little girl who had so often trailed after Mrs. Weadick; they were the worn hands of the grown ranch woman she had become. She noticed the shine of her wedding ring, then looked sideways at Mrs. Weadick, who smiled.

"Hi, Norrie," she said, using Lenore's childhood nickname. Tears welled in Lenore's eyes upon hearing this. No one had called her that for a long time. "I see you got married. Who is the lucky man?"

"Roy McLean. We've been married for forty-five years. He's a good man and a great father, and we have three grown sons, and eight grandchildren. And probably more to come."

"Did you teach them how to ride? Do they know where they come from?"

"They sure do, ma'am." True to their heritage, every single one of the McLeans could ride like the wind, do the work of bringing in the cattle, cutting out the calves, roping and branding. It was in the blood—at the 1975 Calgary Stampede, Lenore's brother, Tom Bews, had won the Guy Weadick Award, which is presented annually to the cowboy who best combined accomplishments in rodeo with personality, sportsmanship, and appearance. She didn't tell Mrs. Weadick that there was no award commemorating the achievements of Flores LaDue.

"And how's the Calgary Stampede going, child?" Mrs. Weadick smiled that old familiar smile. From somewhere deep inside, Lenore McLean heard her own voice above the sound of the wind in the trees and answered: "Mrs. Weadick, you would never believe how much it has grown since you left me."

"You mean they didn't cancel the entire thing for lack of money after Guy and I passed away?" asked Mrs. Weadick.

"It's still the same, only much bigger. It has over seven thousand animals involved in dozens of exhibitions, education, and competition events. For many people now, the Calgary Stampede is their only chance to see animals up close and in action, and you probably don't believe that, but it's true. And you know what, Mrs. Weadick? There are about a million people in Calgary. Can you believe that?"

"One million people, child? Can that really be true?" Lenore's earnest face showed her that it was. "Well, I'll be. But time doesn't stand still for anybody. I remember when Mr. Weadick and I were there for the first Stampede, Calgary had about twenty-five thousand people. But by 1950, the year I took you to the Stampede and you met Herman Linder . . . do you remember that, child?"

"Of course I do. I wore those black boots you gave me."

"That's right. Well, by that year, the population of Calgary had grown to a hundred and twenty-seven thousand." She was silent for a moment. "All those people growing up in the city. And now you tell me there are over a million. Never having the chance to live on a ranch, to feel the wind, ride free. In fact, probably most of them never even had the chance to ride a horse. How sad." She shook her head from side to side. "I'd have died without mine."

Lenore began to wonder where Mrs. Weadick had been all this time. Their being together again felt like the most natural thing in the world.

They sat silently together for a while, just like when they used to ride together in the high country years ago. Lenore was feeling once again the peaceful contentment she had known as a child but rarely had as a grown woman. Somehow, now though, she knew that she would feel that peace for the rest of her life.

"And what about the barrel racing? Was I right about it?"

"You sure were, Mrs. Weadick. Women's barrel racing made its debut in Texas at the All Girl Rodeo in 1947, then it became a prize event at the Calgary Stampede in 1979, and by 1996 it was a full rodeo event for women, and the prize money was the same as for the men. A woman named Monica Wilson raised fifty thousand dollars herself as prize money in 1996, and that Stampede began paying barrel racers equally and including them in the Sunday Finals. And the winning purse is now fifty thousand dollars! Can you imagine?"

Then, in a voice so loud she scared herself, Lenore McLean smacked her hands on her knees and yelled: "The Stampede parade! Oh, my God, you should see what you and Mr. Weadick got started. Today there are over eight hundred horses and it is shown across Canada live on television . . ."

Lenore suddenly found herself alone and knew immediately that she had ruined her dream with her loud voice. "Damn it to hell," she said to herself. "I shouted at Mrs. Weadick."

Just then she felt someone slowly moving her cowboy hat off her face. "Where am I and who turned on that sun?" she half muttered as she tried to prop herself up on her elbows.

"Lenore, time to wake up. Who were you talking to, anyways?" said the laughing voice of her husband, Roy, who had arrived for lunch with the work crew.

*L*enore was riding back to the house when her cell phone rang for a third time. Over an hour had passed since she had saddled up and ridden away from the barn, and this was the third time it had rung. She should answer it. She pulled her horse around and held her quiet long enough to answer. How could she have known that that insistent caller was the director of development at the Cowgirl Museum and Hall of Fame, in Fort Worth,

Lenore Bews McLean on the range at her ranch, Longview, Alberta

Leah Hennel

Texas? The woman told her that, along with five other women, Flores LaDue was going to be inducted into the Hall of Fame. She would become one of the 158 women featured in the Hall's grand rotunda.

"It's about time," said Lenore, blinking back tears. "Yes, yes, of course I will be there to accept her award." Then came the usual question; Lenore wished she'd had a hundred-dollar bill for every time someone asked it, because she would have been a rich old lady: "Is it true that Flores LaDue could rope six running horses with a single twirl of her lasso?"

She answered the Texan with the same reply that she always gave: "On foot or on horseback, with ease, grace, and skill."

Lenore McLean had seen it with her own eyes. During World War II, when there weren't many young cowboys available for ranch work, her mother and the Weadicks had all pitched in to help Mrs. Bews move the cattle home from the high pastures in the foothills. She had marvelled then at Mrs. Weadick's way with a rope, which she was only too eager to share with her young friend.

And to this day, she loved the quiet way Mrs. Weadick was discovered, not announced. What a glorious underdog she was! The woman on the cell phone had just finished telling her that some people wait twenty years on the nomination list, but once the directors found out that in more than thirty-one years of performing and competing, Flores LaDue Weadick had never been bested in trick and fancy roping, her name had gone right to the top of the list.

Young women today might find it surprising and even insulting that there used to be a common saying: Behind every great man there is a woman. Those same young women should know that there was a time when women had far fewer rights than men. Imagine—at the time of the first Calgary Stampede, in 1912, Florence did not even have the right to vote and would not have it until 1916. Nevertheless, though the spotlight was on Guy, it cannot be denied that Florence LaDue Weadick played an important role in the establishment of the Calgary Stampede. She certainly recognized Guy's organizational skills and his vision, and she gave him the right encouragement at the right time. She contributed stability and financial management skills, and was also instrumental in the inclusion of aboriginal people in the Stampede. But perhaps most important, by becoming the ladies' world-champion trick roper, she opened the door for generations of cowgirls who would come after her. Indeed, as much as any man, Florence LaDue Weadick played a role in safekeeping for future generations the rich, unique, and magnificent mythology of the West.

Acknowledgements

Wendy Bryden, Lenore Bews McLean, and Flores LaDue
Mikael Kjellström, graphic design by Cliff Kadatz

After mentioning the most important women in my life in my lengthy dedication of this book, I must now thank my kindly husband, Ian, our four handsome sons: David, forty-five; Patrick and Michael, forty-one; and especially John Paul, forty-three, who, as my long-suffering technical advisor, seemed immune to pain. Hugs and kisses to our three grandsons, Bob, Mac, and James, for hanging in with me during the gestation of this book. I really did try to get to all your birthdays.

The subject of this book has fascinated me ever since I was carried on my father's shoulders on his annual search for a good location to watch the Calgary Stampede parade. As I watched curbside, surrounded by our family, I forever looked for cowgirls among the parade participants, but there weren't many in evidence in those early days. So when I met Lenore Bews McLean in 2002 and realized that she was the real deal and had ridden in many parades, I was delighted that she agreed to open her life to me through her vast library, interviews, scrapbooks, photographs, postcards, and diaries.

Every chapter in this book has been formed by the hospitality of Lenore and Roy McLean and my inspirational road trips to their Longview ranch, located at the foot of the superlative Rocky Mountains of Alberta.

Being a rancher's wife with three grown sons with wives and families, plus raising cattle and horses was complex enough for Lenore, but in May 2005 her husband got bucked off his horse and was airlifted to Foothills Hospital, in Calgary, where he was out cold for seventeen days in the intensive-care ward. This terrible event caused much uncertainty. Happily, though, many people helped Roy McLean make a total recovery. And all the while, I was eternally grateful to the man who cheered this book on—Kevin Hanson, my Alberta-born publisher, who is now president of Simon & Schuster Canada. I owe Kevin an enormous vote of thanks for making this book possible—publishers who can bring a manuscript from languishing in a kitchen drawer to the light of day are pure gold. This would pretty much describe Kevin Hanson, whom I first met in 1987, when he was working for Canada's own publishing legend Mel Hurtig, of Edmonton, Alberta. When Hurtig told me that he would publish my book *Canada at the XV Olympic Winter Games*, he said that his vice president, Kevin Hanson, would phone me. He did, and his first words to me were: "Talk to me." And here we are, over twenty wonderful years later, still talking, but this time it is to you, dear reader. Alison Clarke, also with Simon & Schuster Canada, has had a lot of fun with the creation of this book. My editor, Karen Virag, greatly added to the dialogue and the Calgary component of the story.

This book was partly written around the private family collections belonging to Flores LaDue Weadick and to Lenore Bews McLean, and many of these precious articles have now been donated to the Calgary Stampede and to the Glenbow Museum and Archives. The drawings of some of these items were illustrated by my ethereal niece Penny Munro Reid, a graduate of the Chicago Institute of Art, who now resides with her husband, Paul, and two young daughters in Edinburgh, Scotland.

The thing about books is that they give you a chance to say something. And I'd like to take this opportunity to say something in the way of thanks to all my lifelong friends involved with the Calgary Stampede, past presidents in particular, who encouraged and supported Lenore Bews McLean and me as we began and finished this book together. You are far too many to mention, but you all know who you are.

That being said, I must say a special thanks to my dear friend Colonel (Retired) Desmond Deane-Freeman, age ninety-five, who as an ten-year-old boy living in the Pekisko District witnessed and later described to me Flores LaDue Weadick's performance that was staged by Guy Weadick at the Stampede Ranch for His Royal Highness, Edward, Prince of Wales, in 1923.

Thanks also go to trick roper Ray Lem, who actually performed in Flores LaDue's hand-carved leather and silver championship saddle for a rodeo show season in the 1950s and whose advice on trick riding, roping, and knots proved invaluable. When Ray Lem was offered the use of the saddle by its owner, a former employee of the Bar U Ranch, it was languishing in a crate in a barn in Yellow Creek, Saskatchewan. Eventually the saddle that Flores LaDue Weadick won at the 1912 Stampede made its way back to its rightful place in Alberta and now graces the entrance hall of the Stampede headquarters in Calgary.

I am also grateful to the descendants of three of the Big Four—Don Cross, Dennis Burns, and George Lane—for their continued volunteer contributions to the Calgary Stampede and the Bar U Ranch. The Calgary Stampede's CEO, Vern Kimball, and community partnerships manager, Tracey Read, deserve a medal of honour for being in the saddle with this project since day one. Thanks also go to Calgary Stampede Centennial Strategist Laura Babin, who deftly guided the manuscript through its final chute toward publication.

Another bow goes to Oliver Perry, ninety-two, whose wonderful stories added tremendous colour to this book. We hope to see him riding shotgun in Guy Weadick's 1927 Chevy Capital one-ton truck in the 2012 Calgary Stampede parade.

And for all of our families and our city and country friends who have been asking Lenore Bews McLean and me over the past six years: "When is the hundredth anniversary of the Calgary Stampede?" you won't have to wait much longer.

We'll be looking forward to seeing you at the Greatest Outdoor Show on Earth when the Calgary Stampede celebrates its one hundredth anniversary, July 6–15, 2012.

2005 Alberta Centennial

There is indeed cause for celebration
in the existence and persistence of this
remarkably beautiful and energetic province
—its cantankerousness and its amiability—
its stubborn individualism and its disarming
sentimentality—its fierce competitiveness
and its steadfast belief in community.
From its beginnings, Alberta has stimulated
and thrived upon contradiction, diversity,
spicy variety—depths and heights,
flatness and pointedness, the eternal
and the absolutely brand-new.

—John Murrell, playwright

Bibliography

Byers, Chester. *Cowboy Roping and Rope Tricks*. New York: Dover, 1966.

Coburn, Walt. "Guy Weadick," *True West Magazine*, 20th anniversary issue, 1973.

Collings, Ellsworth, and Alma Miller England. *The 101 Ranch*. Norman: University of Oklahoma Press, 1937.

Curtis, S. Edward. *Native American Wisdom*. Philadelphia: Running Press, 1994.

Dixon, Joan, and Tracey Read. *Celebrating the Calgary Exhibition and Stampede: The Story of the Greatest Outdoor Show on Earth*. Canmore, AB: Altitude, 2005.

East Longview Historical Society. *Tales and Trails, 1900–1972: A History of Longview and Surrounding Area*. Longview, AB, 1973.

Evans, Simon. *Prince Charming Goes West*. Calgary: University of Calgary Press, 1993.

Forster, Merna. *100 Canadian Heroines: Famous and Forgotten Facts*. Toronto: Dundurn, 2004.

Gray, James H. *A Brand of Its Own*. Saskatoon, SK: Western Producer Prairie Books, 1985.

Gunderson, Harald. *The Linder Legend: The Story of Pro Rodeo and Its Champion*. Calgary: Sagebrush, 1996.

BIBLIOGRAPHY

Hurtig Mel. *The Canadian Encyclopedia*. Edmonton, AB: Hurtig Publishers, 1985.

Kelly, Leroy V. *The Range Men*, 75th anniversary ed. High River, AB: Willow Creek, 1988.

LeCompte, Mary Lou. *Cowgirls of the Rodeo*. Chicago: University of Illinois Press, 1993.

Livingstone, Donna. *The Cowboy Spirit: Guy Weadick and the Calgary Stampede*. Vancouver: Douglas & McIntyre, 1996.

MacLaren, Sherrill. *Braehead*. Toronto: McLelland and Stewart, 1986.

National Cowgirl Museum and Hall of Fame. http://cowgirl.net/home/.

Nelson, Doug. *Hotcakes to High Stakes*. Calgary: Detselig, 1993.

Patterson, R. M. *Far Pastures*. Sydney, BC: Gray's Publishing, 1963.

PBS. *The West*, "Frederick Jackson Turner" www.pbs.org/weta/thewest/people/s_z/turner.htm. (accessed September 28, 2010).

Poirier, Thelma. *Cowgirls: 100 Years of Writing the Range*. Red Deer, AB: Red Deer College Press, 1997.

Regular, Keith. *On Public Display*. Vol. 34, No. 1, Historical Society of Alberta, 1986.

Savage, Candace. *Born to Be a Cowgirl: A Spirited Ride Through the Old West*. Vancouver, BC: Greystone, 2001.

Shiels, Bob. "Calgary: A Not Too Solemn Look at Calgary's First 100 Years." *Calgary Herald*, 1974.

Ward, Tom. *Cowtown*. Calgary: McClelland & Stewart West, 1975.